How to Make a

Good Living

as a

Professional
Psychic

How to Make a

Good Living

as a

Professional
Psychic

Cover photo by Joe Nicols

Illustrations by Karuna Eve Nicols

International Standard Book Number:
0-9666436-0-7

Library of Congress Catalog Card Number:
98-090750

Published in 1999 by

To my loving wife Karuna, for her inspiration and encouragement;

To my friend and office manager Diana, for her unwavering support;

and to my children, Heather and David.

TABLE OF CONTENTS

INTRODUCTION

If you would have predicted even 15 years ago that I would become a full-time professional palmist and psychic, I would have laughed and told you not to quit your day job. I could not even have imagined it. But guess what happened.

Since my first year in college I have been an enthusiastic metaphysical hobbyist, having had fun dabbling in palmistry, astrology, past life exploration, tarot, reading the regular deck of cards, dream interpretation, interpreting jewelry and clothing, and a lot of other juicy stuff. However, during the first 17 years I did psychic readings, I was unwilling to consider being a professional psychic, that is, taking money. I did readings for free for people who had heard of my interests. I never solicited clientele, and I stayed "in the closet" while pursuing a more acceptable "straight" profession like speech pathology.

So, 15 years ago I was working three jobs as a speech therapist to support my family and struggling financially. As I continued doing free readings on the side, various friends began shoving money into my hands after receiving their readings, and encouraging me to think about doing this psychic stuff for a living. I had every logical reason not to go public. I thought, "This stuff is weird and people will think I'm weird . . . I'm not really that good, if I take money I have to be good . . . I don't want to feel responsible for others . . . I probably can't make a living at this." And so on.

For three years I took money for off-duty readings. In my day-time job, however, I was feeling progressively more trapped and emotionally fried. Finally I decided to take the big leap and blow off my programmed childhood fear about being different. I was determined to try doing publicly and professionally what I loved to do anyway, even if I didn't get paid for it. My metaphysical friends were supportive, but my "straight" and medical friends responded by saying things like "You're going to do *what?*" and "Nobody makes a living at *that!*"

I was very nervous about the whole prospect of leaving a good traditional job and going into the unknown. What if I couldn't make it and had to crawl on my belly back to my previous career? At least I could conceive of that possibility. What was not clear at the time was how I could be successful at this new psychic work, and what would happen in the future. (Yes, I could see better for others than for myself.)

Now, some 15 years after having gone public, I can see how through trial, and in some cases error, I have created a successful full-time psychic business. For several years now my practice has grossed over $100,000 annually, or about four times the income I used to make as a speech therapist.

I have since childhood been interested in strange things like Loch Ness monsters and Sasquatches. I listened to the show *X Minus One* on the radio in the 50's, and watched *The Twilight Zone* on T.V. in the 60's. I also had a vivid imagination, knew things others around me did not seem to know, and had what I now recognize as past-life flashbacks in my childhood and my teens. I kept most of this to myself, usually telling no one, with the exception of my grandmother who also had interests in those weird paranormal areas.

I first met a professional psychic at age 16, when I found "one of them" for my father to consult about job concerns. She impacted me powerfully, and I continue to pass some of her wisdom on to my clients to this day.

I had my first connection with palmistry as a freshman in college. A dorm-mate and I were at our desks writing papers when a guy came in the door and showed us a book of palmistry from the university library. We all joked and played around with the diagrams in the book, comparing our hands to the pictures. I then continued writing my assignment, and the book was on its way back to the library.

The next day, to my surprise, I realized that I seemed to be able to remember everything I had seen in the book the night before — lines, meanings, everything. Not having a photographic memory, I was, needless to say, shocked, and proceeded to the library to find and check out this book myself. The book, *The Laws of Scientific Hand Reading,* by William Benham, first published in 1898, was, it turned out, considered to be the classic text of rational or scientific palmistry. As I read the book again, I seemed to absorb its palmistry information so quickly that I wondered if I had known palmistry in a previous lifetime. My later past-life exploration indicated that I had indeed been a Gypsy at least once in a previous incarnation.

This initial palmistry experience with the Benham book was definitely the blasting cap that ignited the eruption of my metaphysical interest and expression. I began to do palmistry readings for fellow students, friends and their families, and I was flabbergasted when they seemed to recognize what I told them. I soon experimented with learning to cast horoscopes, read Tarot cards, and read the regular deck of cards. I also began to see what appeared to be past lives around people when I let my mind go blank with that intent.

Following college, I spent the next 15 years pursuing several career adventures, including serving in the Army, immigrating to Australia and working in business, and returning to school in the

U.S. and becoming a speech pathologist. I continued throughout that period to do readings on the side, and over time my awareness expanded into being able to see energy patterns, images and colors around people, being able to do what I call psychic body scanning, and psychically interpreting jewelry and clothing.

I have always held to the basic premise that everyone is psychic to a greater or lesser degree, and this includes you. Developed natural talent is helpful, but I believe my own abilities have continued to grow as I use them seriously and regularly, and yours will, too. Given that all of us have psychic abilities, the first thing you need to have on the road to becoming a successful psychic pro or healer is a genuine, active interest in metaphysics, and/or psychic phenomena. The second most important thing for success in building a clientele is a genuine, active interest in people, and in helping them.

This book is an attempt to give metaphysical enthusiasts basic guidelines on how to succeed in making a good living specifically as a professional reader, but it also has application for achieving success in related metaphysical and healing professions. I specifically chose the words "Good Living" in the title of this booklet for a variety of reasons. Good is one of those emotionally-laden terms like *love* or *democracy* which means something different to everyone. Making a good living can suggest merely receiving a lot of income as in the oft-heard phrase "makin' good money," or it can imply an abundance of both joy and remuneration for your work. I prefer the latter interpretation and I am sure that you do, too.

I have my own business style, of course, and I have presented techniques and approaches that have worked for me. There are no doubt many other ideas or avenues which successful professionals could suggest, so use anything from this book that works for you. This is not really a manual on "How To Be Psychic," although I have included a section in the next chapter on ways to improve your psychic ability. Also, putting energy into creating time slots in your schedule will actually draw people to fill the slots, and your accuracy will improve as you have more people to work with.

1 SO YOU WANT TO BE A PROFESSIONAL PSYCHIC

What is a professional psychic and what does one do? A professional psychic takes money for helping or advising other people through the use of intuitive or extrasensory abilities. There are an endless number of ways psychics do readings to obtain information about the present and future. Here are only a few examples of modalities and types of readings:

• Receiving visual/mental images (clairvoyance);

• Hearing a psychic verbal discourse in the mind (clairaudience);

• Assuming an altered state and allowing a discarnate or disembodied being to speak through the psychic (trance channeling);

• Experiencing thoughts or a knowingness about future situations or their outcomes (precognition);

• Feeling emotions or pain, and tactile or kinesthetic impressions (empathy);

• Touching jewelry or objects (psychometry);

• Predicting through charting the stars (astrology);

• Gaining insight through studying the spiritual numbers derived from dates, names and places (numerology);

• Seeing events in a crystal ball (scrying);

• Gaining psychic information through observing the lines and structures in the hand (palmistry);

• Divining through reading Tarot, the regular deck or other types of cards (card reading);

• Finding water or minerals by "witching" with a dowsing stick, or answering questions by observing the motion of a pendulum with a suspended crystal or other object on the end (dowsing);

• Receiving psychic information which is directly written or typed by the reader (automatic writing);

• Other examples include reading tea leaves; interpreting dreams or daily events; interpreting the viscera of sacrificial and disemboweled animals or humans (historically); reading Celtic runes; throwing coins for the I Ching; reading Chinese fortune sticks; reading the way seashells, sticks or bones fall on the ground or a table; using a Ouija board (which I do not recommend, as the guidance can be accurate at first and then become very negative).

If you visit several psychics who are clear and talented, they might use diverse, unrelated methods, but they will all be fairly accurate, and several may even provide you with some of the same specific information. This is because the Earth plane is not just physical, but multidimensional. There are other levels of consciousness around the physical which operate symbolically and holographically. Just as a sunset can be described beautifully in many languages, the holographic image of the future seems able to be translated accurately by a myriad of receptive psychic techniques, such as the ones listed above. I am not sure exactly how this happens, but it does appear to work.

The likely future outcomes of our present situations and decisions are perceivable on another dimensional level, if we are able to tune into that level and look ahead. Our ability to look ahead into the future is directly related to the degree of psychic ability we possess, which allows us to tap into the level of consciousness which portrays the likely future.

I say likely future because we have a tremendous amount of free will choice that profoundly affects outcomes. I like to use a rug-weaving metaphor to describe past, present, and the impact of free will on the future. The past is the rug that has already been woven and is moving away from the loom. The clear psychic is given the opportunity to view the pattern of the woven rug, and to view the colors of the threads which appear to be on the loom. The psychic, with help from spirit guides, can then make predictions based upon these impressions of past patterns and future potential. The accuracy level of the psychic is a product of their clarity and interpretive skill, as well as present and future free will choice alterations by the client. The clear psychic should generally be accurate, unless the client, like the weaver, makes free will choices that change the rug pattern substantially to create a new pattern in the middle of the rug. The weaver may even cut the threads and stop the weaving process, as in cases where free will creates accidents, diseases or premature death.

While I have seen advertisements claiming 95% to 99% accuracy, no psychic is 100% accurate, or if so, rarely. Depending upon how you measure accuracy (which can be fairly subjective), I would venture to say that a professional psychic needs consistently to be a least 50% accurate. In order to impress clients and get return business, a range between 60% to 80% is necessary. Around 70% to 80% seems in my experience to be about average for successful professionals. Of course, these averages should be taken from contact with dozens or even hundreds of clients.

While we really have no control over what free will choices another person makes, we do have some control over the development of our own psychic and interpretive abilities. In fact, every living thing, and that includes every human, has some psychic ability. Just as there are differing abilities in playing the piano (some of us may be just able to play "Happy Birthday," while others glide through Mozart), people also have differing degrees of natural psychic talent. I consider psychic ability to be a gift from God. I know that many of my own clients are more naturally psychic than I am, they just lack either experience or confidence.

I have in my life experienced events that have convinced me of the existence of reincarnation. Talents we are born with, including intuitive skills, may actually have been developed and refined in previous lifetimes. In the same vein, fear or blockage of psychic ability may be the result of one or more negative experiences with the use or abuse of psychic powers in previous incarnations.

When some people first engage in psychic practices, even though they are enthusiastic, they may still have negative somatic experiences such as headaches, nausea or panic reactions. Others may simply go to sleep, or "go blank," as they struggle to receive something. In many of these cases the person is tapping into a soul memory containing a negative association with past-life paranormal events. I believe some of my clients with present day psychic fears may even have been burned at the stake, beheaded, hanged, assassinated or murdered for their spiritual involvement in a past incarnation.

I have observed that both counseling and past-life hypnotic regression can aid people in releasing these blocks more quickly, but I recommend going to a qualified professional to receive assistance. If counseling or regression are not chosen, or if they do not seem to work, desensitization through meditative and psychic practice can be effective. Releasing resistance to psychic experience is an important part of the process of developing paranormal skills.

While this book is not really a manual on how to be psychic, the following are a few tips for developing your psychic skills:

1. **Meditate** - Meditate every day, if possible. Fifteen to 20 minutes is helpful. There are a number of different styles of meditation and you can receive instruction from a variety of individuals or spiritual groups.

Generally, meditation entails stilling the body and mind to achieve a greater connection with Higher Energy, and to experience what some people have called our inner voice. Find a quiet room and turn down the lights. You can experiment with meditating either in silence or with soothing meditation-type music. While some dedicated meditators enjoy sitting in a Yoga lotus position, I am more comfortable in a chair or on a cushion.

Close your eyes and imagine surrounding yourself with White Light for protection and higher guidance. Affirm to yourself that only information which is in your highest good will be allowed to come through. Some meditators mentally repeat a verbal "mantra," a special or sacred word or name, and some individuals may chant verbal mantras aloud. Others may imagine a visual mantra such as a candle flame, a Cross, a beautiful setting or a sacred Being. I feel some sort of mantra is helpful while one is learning to meditate. A mantra lends structure and helps release the "mind chatter" or extraneous thoughts that bubble out from our daily conscious experience when we become still.

I recommend not fighting the extraneous impressions, but acknowledging them like seeing logs floating down a river — note them, and then let them go by. Then return to your verbal or visual mantra. With practice over time, the mind chatter will be less present and noticeable. If you have what some people call "meditation lice," that is your body begins to itch, then scratch it and relax.

You may have a variety of other experiences during meditation. You may hear words, voices or music, or see in your mind's eye images including scenes, people, various living things, objects, symbols, or color flashes. You may experience relaxing, tightening, tingling, or hot and cold areas in your body, or you might experience stillness with little sensation.

Some people may become very relaxed and wish to go to sleep. I recommend resisting the temptation to nod off, if possible. There is nothing inherently wrong with moving to another level of consciousness to deal with our issues, which is what I believe happens when we go to sleep during meditation. However, we derive more benefit if we can stay conscious as we explore our inner depths. Also, with the exception of trance channeling, where the reader may assume a sleep-like state, metaphysical work is of greater benefit to clients if we are able to maintain full consciousness, even if we are in a somewhat altered state during sessions.

Lengths of meditations vary, and depend upon individual preference. I know some people who meditate at least one hour per day, and some who meditate both morning and evening. I generally recommend a daily meditation of at least 15 to 20 minutes, as many days per week as is possible within the constraints of our modern, technologically complex lives.

If you experience negativity or fear during the meditation, or if you feel bodily discomfort following meditation, remember that you surrounded yourself with light at the beginning of the meditation and are protected spiritually. Imagine a grounding cord extending from the base of your spine all the way down to the core of the earth. Also imagine a beautiful, etheric refill tube coming down from your higher self and affixing to the top of your head at the crown chakra. Then affirm, "I now release anything from my consciousness and my energy field that is not for my highest good." Imagine "flushing" all negativity from your body area and feel the dark, heavy energy flowing out through the base of your spine and down the cord to the core of the earth. Then breathe pure healing light down the tube from your higher self, and into your body area through the top of your head, refilling your entire etheric space. You may feel you need to repeat this technique several times to achieve the desired state of release and cleansing.

2. **Remember to work in the Light** - My position is that everything originally comes from the Light or God, and that nothing is stronger than God's Light. However, I feel that dark energy is also allowed to exist by God's grace, for whatever it teaches us. We all have our own weaknesses, whether they be emotional, psychological, energetic, karmic, etc. As we work with people and emotional situations, we are susceptible at times to being drained (or "energy-vampired") by people, various thought forms, elemental spirits or discarnate beings who seem able to hook into our weakness or vulnerability.

It is amazing how certain clients can catch us off guard, and following sessions they seem to go away feeling great while we feel exhausted. When that happens we have played a role for them which I call "pack mule and gas pump." We have probably just taken on their emotional baggage and we have given them our positive energy. For this reason, always remember to use affirmation/visualization techniques to surround yourself with positive energy, especially before your metaphysical work.

Whatever your deiform — "Light," "God Light," "Christ

Light," "Universal Force," "Oneness," "Light of the Goddess," "Great Spirit," "Manitou," or other (I believe they are all the same) — you need to invoke that protective energy. Experience has taught me the importance of using the previously mentioned technique whereby I surround myself with protective Light, ground myself to the core of the earth, psychically dump or flush negativity to the earth's core, and imagine refilling myself with pure, White Light. Then I imagine any continuing negative energy from the situation deflecting harmlessly off of me and being dissipated, or being grounded straight down to the core of the earth like an electrical discharge. Most of the time, these techniques will energetically perk me back up within less than a minute, and I feel shielded psychically.

It is possible that someone can be very psychic, or a natural healer, but not necessarily spiritual in a positive way. An extreme example is Adolf Hitler, who believed in mystics, used his own psychic energy persuasively, consulted astrologers, and even used mystic symbols, such as the swastika.

If we use our psychic ability without compassion or without a greater spiritual purpose, we run the risk of losing our accuracy level or incurring negative karma which we will have to iron out in this or another life. We have all probably heard the phrase, "What goes around comes around." In other words, what we do positively or negatively will come back to us in one way or another.

This occurs because the Earth plane is a school, a place to learn, love, grow, heal, forgive, live our path, release negativity and express God's Light. The Earth plane is also an incredible cosmic mirror for each of us. We are always working on a piece of ourselves with every person (or client) we deal with. I often tell my clients that I listen to everything I tell them because they are a reflection of a part of me as I am of them. I have an inkling of what I am working on in my own life by what I hear myself saying to my clients all week long. When we are pursuing psychic or healing work, we are increasing our connection with higher energy and accelerating our own spiritual lessons, bringing even more opportunities, choices and challenges onto the path in front of us.

It is also important to try to keep perspective on how much of our work is from us and how much of it is from"Who" we work for. Historically, wherever I have been hassled or confronted by several clients during a short period of time, I have recognized I had been forgetting that I was merely the conduit and that the real guidance was coming through me, not from me.

Many people over the years have commented that we psychics have big egos, and probably necessarily so, considering what we do for a living. However, we need to remember the saying from the Old West: "There never was a hoss that couldn't be rode, and there was never a cowboy that couldn't be throwed." If we become too egotistical, the universal mirror will reflect a difficulty or ego challenge right back in our face.

3. **Expand your professional horizons** — If you are a beginner, get a few different types of readings from professionals, and read books you feel drawn to about the psychic modalities and tools which interest you. You may also decide to take classes from successful professionals in your region. You can usually find these by looking in the advertisement sections of holistic publications, picking up literature at psychic fairs or expos, and asking for recommendations from your metaphysically experienced friends.

4. **Read for strangers or people you do not know well** — It is generally better and easier to read for strangers, for friends of family, or friends of friends. Getting rewarding feedback about information you had no way of knowing builds credibility and confidence. The closer you are emotionally to people, the less objective and accurate you are likely to be. Also, friends and family may hold different metaphysical or religious beliefs, or may not share with you the same understanding and comfort about psychic phenomena and the information which comes through you. They may become fearful, angry, threatened or rejecting.

5. **Experiment with using different psychic tools** — I recommend trying any psychic modalities that feel comfortable. For example, I use palmistry, interpretation of jewelry and clothing, opening to psychic "flashes," physical emotional empathy, reading the regular deck of cards, and a little numerology, whether I'm doing a 10-minute reading at a psychic fair, or a two-hour life reading in my office. Other psychics may focus on combinations such as tarot and astrology, psychometry (holding objects) and psychic impressions, using runes and reading auras, or any conceivable variation. Be willing to use psychic techniques that seem to be accurate, even if they are not your favorite. Accuracy in readings, especially for future events, gets your client's attention and will bring them back another time. So do what you enjoy, but also go with whatever works for your clients.

6. **Receive work from other professionals in the field** — Even if you are an experienced reader, continue to get readings occasionally from other psychics, not only for your own growth and perspective, but also to have a feel for what others in the field are doing. I have probably had at least 10 readings per year over the

past 30 years, and most have been incredibly helpful to me.

7. **Take care of yourself** — Exercise regularly, moderate your diet and periodically get counseling, massages, body work, Reiki or other healing. You need to support yourself and your physical body so you can receive increasingly more powerful spiritual energy and maintain your physical stamina.

In recent years I have discovered that part of my life-long emotional sensitivity seemed to be due to the fact that I was "empathing," or feeling within my own body, the emotions or physical pain of those around me. Thus, it seems that the experiences of Counselor Troi on the old *Star Trek, Next Generation* television show, are absolutely for real. In her case, art imitates life, because it turns out that one does not have to be "Betazoid" to be an empath, as many of us know.

My experience of empathy has been something I have struggled with professionally, as I have tried to balance the benefit of using empathy as a psychic tool, with the difficulty of taking on the pain or stress of others, which can then drain me. I have had to use a variety of visualization techniques, such as the ones noted previously, to protect myself with the Light, and to "dump" or release both my own negativity and the negative energy I may have taken on from others. I also have learned to supplement my energy, often called "chi" (pronounced *chee*) in Chinese medicine, by scheduling myself with Reiki or other hands-on healing treatments, through which I can receive a recharging of my own energetic battery.

If you feel you are improving your psychic skills, you enjoy doing readings, and you have received good feedback from family, friends or other guinea pigs, it may indeed be time to consider going pro. You should at first consider continuing a day job and easing gradually into the psychic bathtub by doing readings part-time, rather than jumping in full-time. Sometimes, whether due to family requirements or past-life karmic unfinished business, we are guided or feel forced to do work for a time that we don't necessarily love. If that is your situation, it is probably in Divine Order, so you have to try to be patient. Hopefully, your patience will be rewarded with a green light from the universe, such as a vision, a job change, a settlement, an inheritance or some other clear message.

Sometimes, however, we do not get a guarantee, and we have to take a big leap of faith. In my case, I avoided becoming a full-time professional psychic for 20 years while I pursued other careers. I went to good psychics myself during the entire period, but none of them ever told me I was going to become a professional psychic. I loved doing psychic work, but when I decided to go pro, I had to walk through the foggy threshold without knowing if I would succeed or fail. At times we just have to go for it. My feeling is that if you love a given pursuit, if you are reasonably good at it, and if you do it regularly and enthusiastically, you will be shown a way to make a living at it.

Once we get to work in what we love, we need to be balanced and not compulsive. We need to honor the requirements of our inner child, our relationships and our family, and honor commitments we have made in our spiritual and social lives, as well. We need to put energy into our work as we break onto the professional scene, but we also need to focus on sustaining growth over the long haul and receiving vital support along the way.

2 SETTING UP SHOP

Places To Work: Where and How

An Office in the Home

Most psychics start their careers by doing their readings part-time in their homes. Many full-time psychics continue to read in their homes as their careers evolve. I read in my home for 17 years as a non-professional, three years as a part-time professional, and my first two years as a full-time professional.

There are some real advantages to a home office. You have the emotional support of and familiarity with your (hopefully) nurturing home environment. You also can have some internal control of the furnishings and work environment. All of your psychic tools are right there and you don't have travel time to and from a work location. There is little or no overhead. You can deal with personal or family situations in between readings. You may even be able to "write-off" as a business expense a separate work room or telephone line.

You can also control the energetic cleansing of your workspace and your home, with techniques such as psychic cleansing, burning Native American smudge sticks, burning incense, playing crystal bowls or Tibetan singing bowls, or using systems such as Chinese Feng Shui (all of which I highly recommend.) One technique for psychic cleansing I like to use entails visualizing your space being surrounded with pure light, and filling your

space with a psychic whirlpool. Imagine the whirlpool circling rapidly and sucking all dark and negative energies from the space and down to the core of the Earth. Opinions differ, but I have always followed recommendations to imagine the whirlpool flowing clockwise.

With Native American smudge sticks, I recommend lighting them so they are smoking, and walk around to the four corners of each room, waving the stick in the air and affirming a blessing and a release of negativity for the space. Put extra focus on spots where people have congregated in the past, such as the kitchen table or dining areas, the living room, and where people have slept, as well as your metaphysical work area. You can follow the same procedure walking around and playing singing or crystal bowls by rubbing them in a clockwise motion.

The use of Feng Shui can be as general or as specific and detailed as you desire. It is best to purchase books with diagrams and practical examples (see Bibliography) and see how it feels. If there is a Feng Shui practitioner in your area you might wish to contact them and see what they say. Widespread use of Feng Shui in the West is relatively recent, so just like with psychics, you should ask around and get recommendations. I tend to use Feng Shui concepts of furniture placement, and the use of mirrors, plants and artwork in my office and home.

There are also potential difficulties in working in your home. One difficulty can be that you are often allowing total strangers into your space. In my experience most clients are nice, balanced people with occasional challenges. However, once in a while someone may come in who is really angry, fearful or disturbed, and who can leave what feels like a black cloud or tar ball hovering in the room. Cleansing steps such as those just mentioned must then be taken to release the negativity from the home.

Other considerations may come up for female practitioners who are working in the home alone. Sometimes prevention is better than cure. If the female reader senses negativity or sleaze when the prospective client is attempting to book, she may need to arrange to have someone else in the house during the session, to make an excuse and politely refuse to do the session, or possibly to schedule the work at another more public location. Family distractions, especially young children, can prove difficult in working in the home. If they are not in day care or with a baby sitter, children may not always appreciate the need for quiet or for self-entertainment. Believe me, there is nothing like hearing the screams of your own beloved child in the next room for breaking the concentration of a session.

Also, the Internal Revenue Service is apparently getting more strict about a citizen's being able to write-off a home office space. I have even heard that the declaration of an office in the home can potentially red-flag your return for an I.R.S. audit. You should check with your accountant or tax attorney about your individual situation.

House calls to clients' homes are done by some professionals. Personally, I do house calls only if my current reading space is not accessible to elderly, physically challenged or homebound clients. With all other individual clients, I prefer to have them come to my space. This reinforces the client's commitment to the reading and establishes credibility or respect for the reading process. I think client commitment and respectfulness, and reader credibility are essential elements in facilitating the client's opportunity to gain maximum benefit from the reading.

A Separate Business Office

For the past 10 years of my full-time professional practice I have worked in an office space. I truly recommend working out of an office once you have built up a clientele which gives you a more regular work flow. An office lends an air of professionalism and success to your business and offers a sense of safety and trust for your clients. You may wish to find a situation where you can share a space with someone or sublease an office within a suite. Working in an office will allow you to separate work from home and give you the opportunity to compartmentalize your life a little and "leave the office at the office."

If you plan to work normal daytime hours, a normal business building will work. Some of my acquaintances have found cooperative business suites where tenants share a conference room or the service of a receptionist or secretary which are built into the rent. In any case, free parking nearby is an important consideration for clients unless you work in a large metropolis such as New York City, where public transportation is commonly used.

If you work odd hours, flex-time, or nights, or you plan to do night or weekend lectures or workshops, it may be important to have your own outside entrance, or some means of allowing clients in and out without you having to let them in and out yourself. Some interior-access buildings close and lock the doors after hours, and you might need to come up with a plan to allow clients ingress and egress. I generally also recommend that a small but comfortable waiting area be available stocked with reading material, including information about your work. You might also consider a small sound system playing soft background music.

If you do get an office it is probably better that you determine that your landlord is okay with what you will be doing in the space. It is better to clear the air with honesty at the beginning rather than be concerned that the landlord will find out and over-react if they happen to be fearful or ignorant about what you do. I would recommend knowing exactly what you are getting and for how long. Ask about who pays utilities, and be careful if you are splitting utilities with other members of the suite. You could wind up splitting with a software company which has electronic equipment, lighting and air conditioning running all the time.

Verify who pays for restrooms or common areas, and double check the square footage of everyone's offices in the suite. Make sure there is a clause allowing the space to be re-let in case you should need to vacate or relocate. Watch out for clauses allowing variable or escalating utility and tax payments, as utilities or taxes in an upscale or growing area may rise more than you expect (just ask me).

Also, you might be presented with a "move clause" which says something to the effect that the landlord has the option to move you within the building or complex at his discretion, if it more easily allows him to fit in a tenant needing a larger space. I carefully choose my offices with respect to the energy and layout (as in Chinese Feng Shui). I prefer not to be susceptible to being uprooted and transplanted to an unknown space which may not be a positive for my work.

Some buildings provide janitorial service, but if not, you may decide it's worth it to clean the place yourself. Specify and verify any build-outs or improvements the landlord has agreed to do, and get *everything in writing* before you sign the lease. Don't be afraid to try negotiating for a reduction of the rent or horse-trad-ing for buildouts or upgrades if you are willing to sign a longer lease. You may, for example, be able to get recarpeting or re-painting included if you are willing to sign a five-year rather than a three-year lease.

Of course, a major downside of having an office is that you incur a regular overhead expense which is there waiting patiently for you each month like a pet waiting to be fed. And it wants to be fed regardless of how many clients you see, or whether you are healthy or ill. It is obviously important to budget a reasonable cushion to cover the rent, and to stay within your means. Don't "go for broke," pledging the family jewels to support your office, and then have to live under either pressure or terror to come up with the money. That kind of distress is cumulative, can adversely affect your health physically and emotionally, and can be disruptive to your family life and the energetic flow of your business.

Basic Equipment and Props for Success

Although I have met metaphysicians who are gifted business people, most of us (myself included) are not always very grounded in being organized for daily business requirements. Given that one is an accurate psychic or successful healer or practitioner, the difference between making a "bare" living and a "good" living can be merely a matter of business organization.

For starters, organizing with good basic equipment is a must. There is an old axiom that "it is a poor workman who blames his tools." But, on the other hand, most professional workmen know the value of having good tools. Having good equipment improves the quality of your work and the chance of your success. Good equipment saves you time, money and aggravation in the long run, and improves your professionalism and credibility in the eyes of your clients.

The following is a sample list of minimal basic equipment necessities for doing professional readings:

• A good quality cassette recorder, or small portable dictating recorder.

• A spare recorder of some sort that can run on batteries for backup, in case the electricity goes out.

• Reasonably good quality cassette tapes in bulk - you can get them at discount stores.

• A good stereo system and meditation music if you guide meditations.

• An accurate clock (wall or desk).

• Business card holders.

• Plastic windows to hold flyers, either table or wall mounted.

• Business cards and brochures or flyers (see Ch. 3: Marketing).

• Computer and programs as needed for your work.

• *One phone line* with call waiting and an answering machine. If you use your telephone for readings, you may need to consider obtaining a separate line on which to do readings, to avoid interruptions or missed calls on your primary number. With *2 phone lines*, have the first with a rollover to the second line if the first is busy, and the second line equipped with call waiting. This effectively turns two lines into three. Use a separate answering machine with recorded messages for each phone line. I have only rarely appeared to have lost a call on line two when three calls come in at the same time and no one is there to answer the phones. Be careful using your second line for faxes as you may miss some calls if the fax is used frequently.

• A phone attachment for recording your voice and the client's if you do phone readings. (You can get them at most electronic shops.)

• A phone receiver shoulder rest to prop the phone next to your ear, if you do phone readings with a regular phone and need to have your hands free.

• A box of tissues (for your clients, and for you if you are empathic.)

• A good lamp or other light source, with extra bulbs.

• A nice table to work on.

• Chairs for you and your clients.

• Chairs for a waiting area, if you have one.

• A table cloth or decorations.

• A portable electronic fan in case the air conditioning goes out.

For Healers or other practitioners, you might also need:

• A serviceable massage table with appropriate attachments and bolsters.

• Several sets of sheets or towels.

• Candles.

• Optional incense burners.

• A clothing rack or suitable hangers.

• Business cards or flyers from referral sources such as counselors, and Oriental, Naturopathic or medical doctors.

Bookkeeping

Bookkeeping can be tedious or satisfying depending upon your personality. If you know how, and can do your own book work, fantastic! Fortunately, I have been blessed during my past 15 years of professional psychic work with having had office managers who are much better at keeping up with details than I am. A good office manager who can handle the books and who is also able to deal pleasantly with the public is a true gift.

A skilled office manager or bookkeeper should also be able

to assist you in setting up your accounting system and procedures. Here are some suggestions from my experience:

1. Set up a manual ledger or a computer program to keep your financial records. There are reportedly a number of good bookkeeping software packages these days, and my sources have recommended programs such as Lotus 123©, Quicken©, MAS 90©, Peachtree© and Money Talks©.

2. If you can afford a CPA, they may be able to help you set up categories which will fit directly into sections of the Form 1040 for year-end income tax filing. I have found that because I cannot keep up with the constantly changing tax laws, my decision to hire a CPA has saved me money and paid for itself every year.

3. I have preferred to have a separate checking account for my business, and I keep a separate credit card which I use for business purchases only. I also maintain a business savings account, into which I put a portion of my income each month to cover my required quarterly estimated federal tax payments. This is extremely important in order to avoid April I.R.S. panic. In states such as Texas where psychic work is considered an amusement, you may also be required to obtain a sales tax permit and collect and report sales tax.

4. You or your staff member should try to stay caught up by entering regularly, financial information and client names and addresses into your data base and financial program. You might, for example, enter the names and addresses as you process address cards or checks for depositing. Remember to "back up" your updated mailing list and financial records frequently onto a

separate disk in case your computer melts down or erases your database. You also might have a separate back-up disk which you keep outside the workplace in case of fire, burglary or other calamity.

5. Put together an organized schedule for you or your helper to follow. The following are excerpts from the office procedures manual put together by my office manager, Diana:

Monthly Income/Expense — List all monthly expenses (vendor, amount, date to pay). Put recurring annual expenses (i.e., insurance renewals, accounting fees, taxes, etc.) in the calendar so you will know what the upcoming expenses for each month will be. Sub-total monthly expenses. After totaling monthly expenses, add personal salary requirement for a final total. Using the ending balance from the previous month, listed as the balance forward, add the approximate weekly scheduled income, add income from psychic fairs or workshops. Then total the income.

Balance Check Books (Business and Savings) — When the monthly bank statements come in for the business, savings and checking accounts, balance both statements and file.

Paying Monthly Bills — Use the monthly Income/Expense sheet to pay bills. Using this list will help ensure that all bills get paid and paid on time. Write the check, making sure to note what the check is for, account number, etc. on the check and enter it in the check register. Mark the invoice with the date paid, the check number, the amount paid and then file for tax purposes.

Bookkeeping (Business Expenses) — At the end of the month, using check register and the paid invoices from the current months file, post in the expense ledger, each expense under the appropriate accounting source (i.e., telephone expense goes under Utilities/Telephone, office space rent goes under Rent/Seminar) Occasionally a Visa/MasterCard bill will have several different accounting sources which will have to be separated by source. The "Misc." accounting source is for items such as banking fees, artwork for office, insufficient funds, refunds, etc. If there is another business venture, use a separate ledger for those expenses. At the end of the year, compile a ledger sheet of the totals for each accounting source. This ledger will be used to complete the worksheet provided by your CPA for income tax purposes.

Bookkeeping (Business Income) — At the end of each week post all income in the income ledger, by day, for the week (including work from Saturday and Sunday at a psychic fair or workshop). Post how paid, if by cash, check, credit card, gift certificate, etc. This ledger will be used to complete the worksheet provided by your CPA for income tax purposes.

Bookkeeping (Employee Payroll) —

1. Keep track of daily hours on a monthly ledger sheet, counting all sick, vacation, and comp time used or earned.

2. Payroll can be done weekly, bi-weekly, semi-monthly or monthly. On the ledger, post gross wages. Using the Internal Revenue Service Circular E, Employers Tax Guide for the current year, calculate Federal Withholding, Social Security and Medicare taxes based on gross salary. Deduct Federal Withholding, Social Security and Medicare (or any other deductions such as insurance or advance) from the gross salary for the net salary.

3. Payroll liability is employer's portion of taxes deducted from employee's salary. Each year the Internal Revenue Service determines the percentage for employer's liability for FICA and Medicare. Take the gross salary times the percentage for FICA and the percentage for Medicare plus the Federal Withholding, which equals the amount of employer liability for the month to be made in the 941 payment to the Internal Revenue Service. The IRS determines whether you will make quarterly, monthly or weekly deposits. These payments are generally made to your banking establishment with a 941 coupon. Write a check in the amount of the final employer's liability and put the Employer's Identification Number and the quarter of the payment on the check.

4. At the end of each quarter a 941 Quarterly Report must be completed and sent in by the last day of the month following the end of the previous quarter (i.e., quarter ending March, the report has to be postmarked by April 30.) When you have an Employer's Identification Number, generally you will automatically receive the report in the mail, but in case you do not receive your report, call the IRS at 1-800-829-3676 to ask them about the quarterly report. It is your responsibility to make sure that all quarterly reports are filed on time.

5. FUTA Liability. Quarterly deposits have to be made as determined by the IRS. The IRS sets a limit of liability per calendar year for each employee. If the limit of liability does not exceed an amount predetermined by the IRS, you may only have to file FUTA reports once per year. If you do not receive the report by the first quarter of the year, call the IRS to determine reporting dates. Again, it is your responsibility to assure that reports are filed on time.

6. Employer's Quarterly Report is a report to the Employment Commission of each individual state. For information about

required reports, contact your state's Employment Commission.

If you have a separate business office, you may need additional office equipment, such as a printer, a disk drive to back up the data base, an electric pencil sharpener, surge protectors, and so on. You probably will also need office supplies, furniture, art for the walls, lighting (if you want incandescent light as I do) and liability insurance to cover your office and clients.

Insurance

Health Insurance

I consider medical coverage to be the bane of the self-employed in the U.S.A. If you don't have health insurance, you should consider canvassing insurance agencies for an affordable policy which at least covers major medical. This is especially true if you are a single parent. Find the largest group within which you may belong, such as "small business owners," and get the most long-standing and reputable insurance company your medical history will allow.

I have been "squeezed out" of insurance by one company who started jacking up the premiums 25% every quarter. Then the next company with which I enrolled would not accept for two years, my family's pre-existing medical conditions which had occurred during the period covered by my terminated policy ("Catch 22"). Being stuck with serious or multiple medical conditions can put you into a state of financial indebtedness which can seem like a personal prison. This may also put a wet blanket on your joy and enthusiasm for helping your clients.

The moral of the story is, if you can't get covered through a job or your partner's insurance plan, get the best policy you can as early as you can, and prepare to stick with it. Otherwise, especially if you have kids, your financial future may seem to be on thinner ice. Ear tubes, long illnesses, broken bones or other injuries can take a serious financial chunk out of your lifestyle potential if you are without insurance.

Other Insurance

If you have a business office, many commercial landlords will require you to carry a fire and casualty policy for your office. I feel this is beneficial and can lend you peace of mind in case of disaster.

3 MARKETING

As soon as you decide to go professional, spring some money for business cards. You might also meditate or use some other method to receive or create a striking logo which together with your name will express your positive spiritual and professional energy. If your logo is incredibly catchy, you may at some time wish to protect it by registering it with your state government as a "service mark," and have Ⓢ printed with your logo. Include on the card your professional name, something succinct about what you do, and a working phone number. Make sure you have a functioning answering machine or voice mail on the phone line.

Consider printing up handbills or flyers with your basic information and more detail about what you do. While I believe personal experience and word-of-mouth tend to be the primary draws for prospective clients, it is important to have something about yourself to hand out wherever you do your readings. This will help reinforce the clients' remembrance of you and will appear to them to be very professional.

If you are creating a flyer about your readings or upcoming professional activities and considering doing a mail-out to your clients, speak to a printer or knowledgeable person about the best and most economical way to do it. The many options you'll be faced with will include: front side only or front and back; letter size; legal size or post card; one-fold or two-fold; white stock or color stock; black print or color print; printed, copied, color-printed or four-color process brochure; first class or bulk mail;

and so on. Some of the above choices are a lot more expensive than others. Put some time into figuring out the best combination for your needs.

I suggest putting whatever the post office recommends, such as "Return Service Requested" on the return address section of your flyer in order to update your mailing list. Remember to "build in" the cost of receiving a stack of address corrections back from the post office. At the time of this writing, each returned item costs the value of a first-class postage stamp. More about this later in the discussion about mailing lists.

I suggest creating a one or two paragraph "media bio" for a media packet. In other words, come up with a one-page personal biography which mentions any credibility-building personal achievements, experiences, recognition or education. Emphasize your metaphysical experience, including how long you have been doing your work, and what you are doing now. If you have done metaphysical work in cities in several states or have worked outside the U.S. (Mexico or Canada qualify), don't be afraid to cite your "national" or "international" experience.

Put the bio together with a business card and any current flyers or advertisements to create the media packet. This packet will then be available for individuals who may invite you to be on radio or television, to work at a high profile party, or to do a public workshop or lecture. It will be much easier for them to know who you are and to grease the skids for your appearance. Be sure to keep the media bio updated.

You might consider putting an ad in the yellow pages or in high profile local holistic magazines. I personally don't tend to get a lot of clients through these avenues, but they are great for keeping your name in front of the public and letting people know that you are around. And I have had clients for whom I have read years previously who upon seeing my name in the phone book or in a magazine decided to book again. Be careful about agreeing to advertise in psychic or holistic directories, though, especially if they are new to the area. They can be expensive, and I have not found that they generate many (if any) new clients.

The advertising "bottom line" is important, especially if your finances are limited. Steward your resources and try to weigh your cost against benefit. While advertising may sell products, word-of-mouth seems to me to be more successful for selling metaphysical services.

If you decide to advertise in newspapers, magazines, brochures or newsletters you will probably be required to make your ad "camera ready." Camera ready means different things to different printers, so check with your printer about their specific requirements. If you include a photo in your ad, you may need to have it digitized. In any event, give yourself enough time to submit the finished ad before the publication deadline.

I have included some samples of a workshop flyer (front and back), publication ads of differing dimensions and a post card mail-out. See figures 1, 2 and 3.

Figure 1 (front) — FLYER

Workshops by: Joe Nicols, M.A.
Psychic and Palmist
Since 1966
Austin, Texas

PALMISTRY (Basic/Intermediate/Advanced)
7:15pm to 9:30pm   Limit 24 People   Fee: $30 Advance/$35 At Door
Friday, May 22, 1998

Joe has over 31 years experience as a Palmist and a teacher of palmistry. In this workshop he will point out the basic lines and structures in the hand which yield specific information about areas such as love-life, career, finances, psychic ability, health, travel and past-life influences. Some intermediate and advanced techniques will be included. A question and answer period will give you the opportunity to learn about your own hand and the hands of others in the group. Please bring a bright flashlight with you. Visual aids and handouts will be provided.

DREAM SYMBOLS - WAKING AND SLEEPING
7:15pm to 9:30pm   Limit 24 People   Fee: $30 Advance/$35 At Door
Thursday, June 11, 1998

This workshop will help you take advantage of the guidance that is constantly available to us all. Solutions to our daily problems and clues about the future can be found in the symbols in our dreams and in the events of our daily lives. Recognizing and understanding those symbols gives us daily guideposts to follow, keeping us on target in fulfilling our life's goals, and achieving our success. Participants are encouraged to bring a dream or recent significant life event, which they can share and interpret during the workshop. A meditation exercise will also assist us in achieving clarity and guidance.

PSYCHIC DEVELOPMENT MINI-WORKSHOPS (Beginning and Intermediate)
7:15pm to 9:30pm   Limit 20 People   Fee: $30 Advance/$35 At Door
Wednesday, July 1, 1998

Through guided meditation, and assistance from your Spirit Guides, you will be using practical visual/physical techniques, including meditation, psychometry (using objects), music and guided visualization, to give you an edge in making decisions for yourself and others. This skill has application in every area of your life. Come to this workshop with current decisions or choices in mind. This workshop is open to beginners and those with previous psychic development workshop experience, or individuals who have already been doing psychic work.

ALL WORKSHOPS AND CLASSES WILL BE HELD IN JOE'S OFFICE AT
1406 CAMP CRAFT DR., SUITE 108, AUSTIN, TEXAS
Space is limited so advance registration is recommended. For further information call 512/328-8118.

Joe Nicols is an ordained minister of the Universal Life Church.

REGISTRATION FOR WORKSHOPS/CLASSES

Name_____Phone(h)_____(w)_____
Address_____(Street)_____(City)_____(State)_____(Zip)
I will attend the following workshops by Joe Nicols:

Workshop Title	Date	Workshop Title	Date	Workshop Title	Date

OR _____ I will attend the Reading the Regular Deck of Cards Class, Fridays, July 10-July 31, 1998
May Joe put you on his confidential mailing list?   Yes   No   Amount enclosed $_____
Please complete registration form and return with check payable to: Joe Nicols
1406 Camp Craft Dr., Suite 108, Austin, TX, 78746

Figure 1 (back) — FLYER

(FIGURE 1-back)

READING THE REGULAR DECK OF CARDS

This four-week class will give you the skills to assist you in gaining insight for yourself and others in the following areas:

Love Relationships	Career decisions or other choices	Time Predictions
Financial Predictions	Two or more direction choices	Geographic moves

Joe has been reading the regular deck of cards for 28 years, and uses this skill daily in his full-time professional practice. He has trained other individuals who are now using their card reading skills as professional psychics in the Austin area and elsewhere. Attendees will receive a certificate following successful completion of the course.

The classes will be held **Friday evenings, July 10, July 17, July 24, and July 31, 1998, from 7:15pm to 9:30pm.**

The fee for the four classes will be $165. Because of limited enrollment, the class tuition will be non-refundable after July 6, 1998. Advance registration is required. Attendees need to bring, to the first session, a deck of regular playing cards that have surfaces which can be written on in pen (i.e., not plastic laminated).

Return Service Requested.

Nicole' Consultations
1406 Camp Crnt Rd., Suite 106
Austin, Texas 78746

44

Figure 2 — PUBLICATION ADS

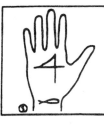

Figure 3 — POST CARD

Greetings:

Good News! I will be returning to Hong Kong from September 6, 1994, through September 23, 1994, and will be doing private readings, lectures and workshops.

Thursday, September 8	7- 9 pm.................*Free Evening With Joe*
Saturday, September 10	10:30 am-5 pm......*Psychic Development Workshop*
Monday, September 12	7 -9:30 pm............*Discovering Past Lives*
Tuesday, September 13	7-9:30 pm...........*Psychic Healing*
Saturday, September 17	10 am-12:15pm....*Psychic Development Mini-Workshop*
Thursday, September 22	7:30-10 pm.........*Psychic Interpretation of Clothing and Jewelry*

Please Contact the New Age Shop at 810-8694 for information about scheduled lectures and workshops, or if you or someone you know would be interested in scheduling a private reading. For personal sessions, cash is preferred, or uncrossed checks, thanks.

I am looking forward to my upcoming visit to Hong Kong and hope I can be of service to you again. Thank you for your support.

Sincerely,

Joe Nicols

Any successful direct mail entrepreneur knows the value of a mailing list. Today's professional metaphysicians are no exception. Always ask permission to put clients on your private mailing list. If they felt benefited by your work they will generally accept, unless there is potential flack on the home front with family members who are opposed to or fearful of healing or psychic subject matter. It is vital to create, expand and regularly update your mailing list.

After I had been reading part-time professionally for about six months, I had developed a confidential mailing list of about 180 people. That first holiday season I purchased boxes of inexpensive generic holiday cards and individually signed my name and a simple "Best Wishes for the Holidays" note on each card. I also enclosed a business card. I found that a number of people called for appointments following the holidays directly as a result of receiving the card. By the second holiday season my mailing list had expanded to the point where sending individual cards was approaching my limit of economic feasibility. After that I sent out flyers about my work or classes.

I recommend that, as your clientele and mailing list grow, you use computer data base-generated mailing labels, and move slowly to a bulk mail mode. You might want to have a mailing service do the bulk mail, depending upon your time, finances and equipment. I suggest placing "Return Service Requested" on your mail-outs in order to upgrade your mailing list. This may incur more cost for returned mail, but it will save time and financial wastage in the future.

I honor my clients' needs for confidentiality. I do the same with respect to my mailing list. I have never and will never sell my list. I feel there is enough invasion of privacy in our technological world as it is. Also, I feel an ethical, professional and spiritual commitment to my clients to do what I say I will do. Maintain control of your mailing list. Consider carefully before you loan either your list or data-base to someone else. I find most printing companies or bulk mail services are reputable and will give assurances about the protection of your mailing list. However, in joint business ventures, I have usually generated my labels and then given them to the other party to be placed on their mail-outs. I feel being careful and protective of my clients' needs for confidentiality keeps my professional energy clean, and contributes to my receiving more success and fulfillment in return.

During the past 15 years, psychic fairs and metaphysical expos have grown from almost non-existent to prolific. Psychic fairs are a great way for practitioners to obtain experience and gain exposure to new prospective clients and to the general public. I have found that metaphysically or holistically oriented events have a good chance of drawing clients who are already motivated to receive benefit from a reading. Other types of conventions or trade shows, such as singles expos or job fairs, may still be successful for you as a reader if enough attendees show up and have the time and money to experience a reading.

Whenever you attend metaphysical events, especially psychic fairs or expos, have plenty of business cards, flyers, brochures and a card or sign-up sheet for your mailing list. These types of gatherings represent your target client population, and offer terrific marketing opportunities. I have attracted many long-term clients through brief initial contacts such as 45-minute lectures or 10-minute readings at psychic fairs and expos.

During the past several years I have also given out business card refrigerator magnets to clients I have read for either at events or in my office. This has worked very well for me. Some practitioners give out pens or pencils labeled with business monograms, and I must say I tend to see their name almost every time I pick up the implement to write. Let's face it, most people like free stuff, and the best free stuff is that which is useful to them. You should seriously consider any offers to make radio or television media appearances. I have often heard marketing people express generalities such as, "There ain't no bad publicity." I can think of exceptions, but for the most part the saying holds true. Even when you experience skeptical or adversarial people during the media event, your name recognition is enhanced, and you will be reaching some members of the audience who are predisposed to be open to your views. In life I find that you can't please or reach everyone, and not anyone agrees with everyone. So the best thing to do is simply to go ahead and do your thing.

Interviews, news specials, call-in talk shows, metaphysical cable access programs, public service announcements and advertisements are all fair game. Make sure to return media phone inquiries promptly as media producers often come up with spur-of-the-moment projects, such as before Halloween, before or during a well-promoted media premiere [as around the movie *Ghost*], or following high profile national or international events (UFO sightings, miraculous sightings of the Virgin Mary).

When you arrive at the production location, always offer the producer your media information packet (media bio), which explains your background and current activities. Be ready in advance with a concise verbal description of what you do or what you are promoting, and a number of questions about your work which the interviewer may ask. If you are doing readings, have a format which lends itself to specific questions or short answers. Media interviewers sometimes ask questions "off the top of their head," or that are complex or difficult to address quickly or easily. A rock music D.J. once asked me to interpret a caller's dream in about five seconds. Give it your best shot and don't be afraid to point out that a specific question is complex, or that it would take more time to answer.

If you have approval from the media staff, remember to give a phone number where you or whoever you are representing can be contacted. Remember to request a cassette copy of the radio show or a videotape containing your portion of the television spot. I generally have had only a few calls or clients generated from each media exposure I have taken part in, but as I said, it's great for continued name recognition.

You may wish to accept every media invitation you receive, but I tend to favor information programs rather than shows with a pure entertainment format. For example, if you are doing interviews or readings on pop-music shows with D.J.'s whose format is comedy, your work may be made light of and not taken seriously. I've had this happen, and I didn't enjoy the experiences. But, as I said, there probably is not any bad publicity, and I have seen clients who reported first having heard me years before on a particular radio show which I felt was awkward or unrewarding.

4 DEALING WITH CLIENTS

Booking Clients

When you are ready to begin your professional practice, create a slot of time during your week which you wish the universe to fill with clients. Decide upon the length of the sessions you are going to provide. I offer 30, 45, 60 and 120-minute readings, and a 90-minute session for psychic development. I charge a different set rate for each length of reading, which I tell the client when they inquire. I find most clients like a choice of services which they can tailor to their own time, resources and needs. Keep a computerized appointment book or planner and update it immediately upon booking clients or changing appointment times.

Keep all professional engagements on your appointment calendar, double check the dates and times and leave reminders for yourself. Due to an administrative error, I once missed a professional event I had agreed to work on a Saturday, and did not realize I had "blitzed" it until Monday. I was thoroughly embarrassed. I fired off a letter of apology with an offer of complimentary readings to the host, but of course never heard from him again. Screw-ups do happen even if we try to be careful, and the best damage control is an honest apology and an offer to accommodate.

Have a verbal blurb ready to give clients when they call for appointments. I tend to ask first if I have read for them before, or how they heard about my work, and if they have ever had readings before. I then tell them how long I have been doing psychic work, and what part of town my full-time office is in. I say that I work by appointment only and I do different lengths of readings, and that they will receive a tape of the session at the end. If the client wishes to know what I do, I give them a brief summary of the types of psychic tools or modalities I use and what those techniques reveal. I then give them the lengths of readings and corresponding fees, and specify that I accept cash or checks.

If the client seems unsure, I suggest that they might think about booking and call back later. If they are ready to book, I ask them what days or times they need and inform them of my available slots. We agree on a time and fee, and I ask for their first and last name. Only a handful of clients have given me only their first name or initials. That usually red-flags their trust issues for me, but I generally go along with their desire.

When they have booked I repeat the date, day of the week and time, let them know that my office manager will call to confirm, and suggest that if any conflict or a change of plan occurs, to please let me know so that I can offer the slot to another client. I suggest always getting a phone number from clients when they book in order to confirm their appointment, or in case you become ill or have an emergency, and need to re-schedule for your own purposes. If you are full-time or very busy, you may even consider keeping a cancellation list of people who wish to get in immediately and have flexible schedules.

Doctor and dentist office staff who call patients to confirm appointments really know what they are doing. I see roughly 25 to 35 clients per week in my office. I have estimated that I would lose about 20% of my business due to client scheduling conflicts, emergencies or just flat no-shows if my office manager did not call to confirm. If you are able to learn in advance that a client is not coming, you have more of a chance to refill the slot.

If you decide to confirm bookings, make sure you tell the client that you or your assistant will call them to confirm at the telephone numbers they give you. Then I recommend calling them or leaving a message to confirm their appointment a day or two in advance of their visit. Some clients ask that you not reveal the nature of the confirmation on the answering machine or to the person who answers the phone. You can ask them to call you in advance to confirm, or if you need to call them, just say you are returning their call to you, or that you are confirming a meeting or appointment.

I must add here that I have found it can at times be awkward if a male practitioner calls to confirm a female client's appointment, especially if the client's male partner answers, and the partner does not know anything about the appointment. I have gotten questions like, "*Who* is this?" and "What is this *about*?" When that happens I try to be polite and businesslike and say something like, "I'm sorry, but I need to talk to Ms. Client about it. Thank you."

In rare circumstances where the client books, but does not give a phone number, does not confirm, and does not show for the appointment, I make a note on my schedule book. If the client calls back to rebook and the same scenario occurs, I thereafter allow a pencil-in booking which is not held unless I receive advance payment.

If a client repeatedly gives their phone number, does confirm, but then cancels or no-shows (three or more times in a row), the next time they call I ask my office manager to inquire as to possible conflicts the client may be having about receiving a reading. On some of these occasions I have also required the client to pay in advance.

Some professionals charge a cancellation fee or a full fee for missed appointments without at least 24-hour prior notice. My inclination is not to focus energy on trying to collect from a no-show, but instead be open to receiving an emergency or last-minute appointment for that slot, or just assume that I needed a break during that period.

I always let clients know my fee schedule when they book. Since I charge for my time, not my gift, I try to make sure my clients get all of the time they are paying for. As such, I almost always run over a few minutes at the end of each reading. I prefer not to bring a session to an abrupt halt or cut short an important issue because the clock has run out. To help me keep to a schedule, I build in extra time between readings to adjust for clients arriving late or my own time overrun at the end of the reading.

I ask for payment in either cash or check, and I do not charge more for extra time I spend on the reading. If a client asks if they should pay for the extra time, I explain that it was my choice to run over, and that the fee is the one I originally stated. If the client insists, I say that a tip is not required, but that I appreciate and will accept it if they wish to offer it. I am comfortable with this process and it reassures my clients that I do not have a mercenary motive for time over-runs.

Some practitioners use a sliding scale for clients whose resources are low. I prefer to offer shorter, more affordable sessions, such as $20 for 10-minute readings at psychic fairs, or arrange for multiple time payments. In a couple of instances where I knew the clients were dead broke, I did not discount the fee but told them to send it when they could. Similarly, when clients forget their cash or checkbooks, I just ask them to bring the payment back and stick it under the door or just mail it in. The vast majority of people have honored their commitments.

Professional Tips in Connecting With a Client at the Beginning of a Session

How we connect with clients is important for their well-being and for the long-term longevity of our practice. It is paramount to be as caring and sensitive (and as ethical) as possible throughout all client interactions. I try to do this by presenting a recognizably safe personal image, discussing with the client what I will and will not be doing, being ready to answer questions about the process (such as those about reader accuracy), maintaining an ongoing awareness of client boundaries and levels of comfort, and being flexible if the client reacts uncomfortably.

I have developed a fairly set pattern of greeting clients at the beginning of sessions. As with booking clients, my normal procedure is to ask the client how they heard about me, and whether they have had a reading from me or someone else before. I then explain generally what psychic modalities I will be using. Next, I give disclaimers such as:

1. I do not predict death, divorce, dire illnesses or crashes, but if I sense those sorts of things, my job is to warn the person that the potential negative outcome is changeable, and that they may take certain corrective steps.

2. I am not a medical doctor and do not diagnose illness, but if I perceive low energy or health difficulties, it is up to clients to refer themselves to a doctor or other professional.

3. I am not a counselor or psychologist, and encourage clients to seek appropriate professional help regarding support with mental or emotional issues.

4. I am not 100% accurate (no psychic is), but I will do the best job I can.

5. I adhere to confidentiality and will not tell anyone what I

tell any client.

6. The client may ask questions at any time, and the reading may be recorded as part of the service, unless it is occurring at a psychic fair or expo, in which case they may record it themselves.

With respect to number four above, I think no psychic achieves 100% accuracy for a variety of reasons, such as exercise of free will choice by the client, misinterpretation by the reader, "bleed through" of someone else's energy into the reading, and "higher" intervention for the greater good of the client. I tell my clients that no psychic can click with everyone, and as they say in professional football, on "any given Sunday" you can have a great day or not fare as well. Accepting that reality, psychics must experience their inner strength, have broad shoulders, and be ready to accept and use negative feedback for personal growth. Generally, if you maintain primary focus on service to your client, good things will continue to happen.

It sometimes helps to have structure with respect to awareness of ethical behavior toward clients. Several years ago I founded and was a member of a non-profit organization called the Central Texas Parapsychology Association. During its 11-year life, the organization promoted metaphysical educational opportunities and psychic fairs, which were open to the public. Member psychics were required to sign and adhere to a 10-point code of ethics. The following four points are excerpts from that code which I feel ethical professional psychics should consider embracing as a part of their ethical commitment to clients:

1. The client must be informed in advance of the total cost and duration of any services before those services begin. Hidden charges, or any creative billing practice that is not completely explained to the client before transaction or exchange of services for any compensation is entered into, are expressly forbidden.

2. A reader shall not abuse a client's naiveté, trust and/or vulnerability in order to benefit financially, sexually or otherwise; nor will the reader provide any harmful or unethical programming or recommendations.

3. No reader may claim their system or process is the one and only means of interpretation of spiritual or psychic information.

4. A reader may not claim to have the guaranteed ability to initiate or discontinue events, including the use of hexes, spells, etc., or possession, exorcism, etc.; nor claim any control of any serendipitous event, including rain, earthquake, etc.

When reading for a client, remember that even if they are skeptical, they will recall much of what you say. Do not be afraid to describe what you see, and try not to discount what you tell them. When something you have said materializes in the future, it will register with them and they will flash back to your reading, and this will bring credibility to your work.

If during or following a reading, I find a particular client is continually shaking their head "no," being confrontational, or expressing doubt about my accuracy, I will stop the reading and try briefly to discuss the situation. If rapport or credibility with the client cannot be re-established, I present the possibility that I may not be able to help them, and that I will be glad to refund their fee and give them the tape of what has already been done. Luckily, this situation has not arisen that often, but it does happen to every professional. I find it is easier and far less expensive to refund the money as cheerfully as possible, thereby defusing a difficult situation, and reducing the risk of an unsatisfied client spreading negative advertising.

Image

You may want to consider developing your professional image. Some psychics prefer a causal look, some dress flamboyantly, and still others dress like business professionals. This decision relates to your personal preference and your clientele.

My preference is to dress as a business professional, especially in public. Some of my clients have occasionally noted at public events that they think I look like I work in a bank. Part of my purpose is to upgrade the image of "psychic" from being a "gypsy" or "fortune teller" (which may conjure up public judgments about being "hokey" or "a side show" or "just for entertainment") to that of a serious and viable professional. Also, I wish to project a "normal" middle-class persona which may relax prospective clients and help them to feel more comfortable and open.

Unless you wish to be identified as a spiritual counselor within a certain faith, I recommend projecting a non-denominational image. I believe God-Light is in every person, and can be found within each religion. I acknowledge and honor my clients' rights to their own background and belief system. People of all faiths get readings. They may be Christian, Jewish, Islamic, Buddhist, Hindu, Sikh, Native American, Wiccan, B'hai, Agnostic, and so on. Before I offer a client a helpful affirmation/visualization, I always ask them what their current religious orientation happens to be. I then use their own deiform in the affirmation such as, "God," "Christ," "Light," "Great Spirit," "Goddess," "Universal Force," or "Whatever."

If you get the occasional religious fundamentalist on the phone or in public (as I have) accusing you of working for the Devil, try not to take it personally and remain calm. I try to respond lovingly with something like "I work for God (or 'the Light'), but thank you for your concern," and on rare occasions I might even add flippantly, "and I thank God for the Bill of Rights in our country which allows us the freedom of our beliefs."

An area of image which might also come under professional ethics is confidentiality about the contents of readings. Trust is an important ingredient of success in a service business. It's often hard to win and easy to lose. Most of my clients are extremely concerned about confidentiality. I do not give out the names of my clients unless someone else knows about the visit and mentions the client's name first. I do not approach clients in public, but let them approach me before acknowledging them. If I use a client situation example in a reading or public presentation, I *never* mention the client's name.

I generally see spouses or family members individually, and I tell them that I will not disclose to them anything I told the other family member or tell the other family member what I told them, unless it specifically comes up in their own reading. If a client is a normal (as opposed to mentally handicapped) 12-year-old or older, I give them their tape and do not discuss the content of the reading with their parent, or with the person that brought them.

Another aspect of image is professional respect from your peers. Try to avoid thinking in terms of competition between yourself and other metaphysical practitioners. I believe that the more work we all do, the better it is for all of us. I also recommend avoiding negative comments about other professionals, since it fosters negative energy and can definitely backlash on you.

I have had a client who once said to me several years ago, "So and so reader told me my husband was going to die of a heart attack." Rather than responding negatively about the reader, I said something like, "Well, I don't predict death, as I believe the decision about that event is made between the person and God, but I don't get that your husband's health is in imminent danger (he's still alive and healthy as of the time of this writing). Another distraught client once said, "So and so reader told me if I have this abortion I will never have children." After tuning into the situation I said, "I don't get that about you, I still see you having a child in the future." If you encounter such situations you can also say something like, "I'm not sure what they meant by that, but let me see what I get," and then say what you feel about the client's situation.

If an occasion arises where another reader has made a stark and direct prediction about your client and you see a similar outcome, take the opportunity to point out ways the client may change their consciousness or behaviors and possibly avoid the negative outcome. Or, you may point out aspects of the greater spiritual lesson which may be playing out, and try to put a positive spin on it. You could say something like, "This situation may look negative, but it is a time of spiritual testing for you, and you will see the light at the end of the tunnel in x number of weeks (or months)." Or you could say, "This period will seem difficult, but you will be healing past pain, learning patience and gaining inner strength. This will pay off in the future as you project more confidence and attract more positive people and situations."

In any event, any professional can have a bad day, and clients can and do misunderstand and misquote readers. It is a courtesy to other practitioners to give them the benefit of the doubt. They will sense your professionalism and will likely return the favor. Reserving judgments with respect to what you hear second- or third-hand about another reader is important.

5 VARIOUS WORK OPPORTUNITIES

Psychic Phone Work

In addition to face-to-face work, I do readings over the phone. Over time I have built and maintained a significant long-distance clientele who have never seen me in person. They generally hear about me through a friend or relative who has come to my office. My procedure is to have prospective clients call to make an appointment for a certain time, taking into account geographical time changes.

The client then phones me at the appropriate time (they pay for the call), I answer and do a 15 to 30 minute reading. I can provide a cassette tape of both my voice and the client's through the use of my phone-tape "gizmo" if they wish to have permanent recording. I generally suggest they get a tape because it provides a record and can be reviewed later. If the tape is requested, I add $5 for shipping and handling above the normal rate. Then I have them post a check or money order. When that fee is received I pop the tape in the mail. I have generally had good feedback about phone work, and clients are often amazed that psychics can be accurate at long distance.

Several of my psychic colleagues whom I respect have worked with 900-number psychic hotlines, and I believe the hotline clients are receiving legitimate benefits from their calls with these individuals. I have heard however, that this "cold-call" type of work with the public can be very tough and energetically draining. Also, I understand that even though the 900-lines may charge clients three to four dollars per minute, the psychic receives somewhere in the neighborhood of 25¢ to 50¢ per minute. I feel the hotlines are a great place to gain pressure experience, and to make some money on the telephone from your home. But if a reader has a regular local clientele they may need to look seriously at the time, money and energy cost/benefit of hotline work.

Psychic Fairs and Expos

Psychic fairs in your local area are usually good because you can attend the event and not incur overnight expenses. If you go out of town, you need to take into account the booth fee, travel time and expense, lodging and food cost. You should compare as well the net financial and energetic benefit of the out-of-town experience with the benefit you would have received if you had stayed home and worked locally during the same time period. Out-of-town fairs can really work if you can economize your travel costs by carpooling or using frequent flyer miles. Staying with friends or family or sharing lodging also helps tremendously.

If you enjoy both traveling and building up out-of-town clients, you may be able to turn a working trip into a working vacation. You of course must realize that all psychics, including myself, have experienced non-productive ("crash and burn") fairs, especially on the road. One needs to try to be philosophic and realize that there is always some risk attendant to these pursuits. Again, you need to look at the cost/benefit of reading at specific events.

When signing up for a psychic fair, you need to know the exact dates, times and location of the fair, the total cost of your space, how much room you will have and the availability of electricity if you need it. You need to know about availability of parking for yourself and clients, when the space will be open in advance to set up, and how long you have following the fair to take down your items. You need to determine the number of chairs, and the number and sizes of tables that will be available, and whether table cloths or skirting will be provided. You should ask about any limitations on the size of signs or if there are wall restrictions on taping or pinning up signs or posters.

Ask what advance advertising will be done for the fair. If the fair is a regular event, ask about the actual attendance at previous or more recent fairs. You may be given an opportunity to have your name listed in the media advertisement. If the fair is on your home turf, or if you already have a clientele in the area, it might be worth it to pay extra for the name recognition, depending upon how tight your budget is.

Some psychic fair operators set a maximum dollar amount and minimum time limit per reading, such as $15 for 15 minutes. Compare the amount per hour (including normal breaks) that you would make at a busy fair, with the amount per hour you would make in your home or office. For example, you might charge $45-$60 per hour at the fair compared with what you charge privately, say $60 per hour. If the money estimation is pretty close, or, if you are a part-time professional, a new reader building clientele, or you just enjoy traveling and working (if the fair is out of town), you may be comfortable with the fee for time limitations of a particular fair.

If your normal private fee is much greater than the estimated hourly fair amount, or you already have a large clientele and business overhead, the time/energy exchange may not be beneficial. In that case you might want to limit your attendance to fairs where you can set your own fee and reading length, such as $20 for 10-15 minutes.

If the fair is out of town, ask the fair operator if you can get a price break on local lodging. Many operators have a deal with the host hotel for a discount or rooms during the event.

In preparing for a psychic fair you need to have a catchy but professional-looking sign. I have a large wooden sign for local gigs and a fold-up cardboard sign for events requiring air travel. You should have table cloths, flowers or other easy-to-transport decorations, plenty of business cards, flyers, information about your work, and a pad of paper or address cards to record mailing addresses. If you need electricity, always take both a short and a long extension cord. Take special care of the tools of your psychic trade and have spares available where it's feasible. Weird things can happen in this business — your lamp can burn out, you can forget your tarot deck, your sign-up sheet pencils can evaporate, or whatever.

If you have decided to attend a psychic fair, you may want to decide in advance whether you need a helper to support you and whether to use a client sign-up sheet. If you are an inexperienced reader you may be comfortable working without an assistant and using a straight sign-up sheet where clients register in order and wait their turn. If you are already an experienced and successful professional, you may want an assistant out front to communicate information, to keep time for you, and to keep the clients moving through. You probably will want to use a set-time sign-up sheet. This will help you to stay focused on your readings and maximize your efficiency and productivity.

If you are receiving cash and need to make change for the readings, it is helpful to bring some cash in appropriate denominations in case your very first client has no change and drops a $100 bill on you. It may be disruptive to your continuity to ask the client to go get change and come back to pay you. If you anticipate a large number of clients, you might also want to bring a small purse, bag or container to hold your change and the fees you receive.

You will need an accurate timer that does not have an obnoxiously loud "beep" which can distract other readers around you. I recommend a small digital timer that keeps track of exact minutes and seconds. You can find these at local department stores or discount houses. If you are very busy, using a beep-timer is much more effective than trying to watch the clock.

Some readers make a complimentary recording of their psychic fair readings. This is a good service for clients, it gives them a record of the information from their visit, and provides marketing and advertising. I generally do 10-minute, back-to-back readings at psychic fairs and choose not to provide a tape, but tell my clients they are free to bring their own cassette recorder.

At least a day prior to an event, I recommend making and checking a list of furniture and equipment items you need to bring, and begin stockpiling them. I have enclosed a copy of the checklist my office manager, Diana and I have compiled to help me prepare for fairs (see Figure 4).

Figure 4 — CHECKLIST

Sample Check List for Psychic Fairs

READER'S TABLE
___ Tools of your trade for readings   ___ Table
___ Extension Cords   ___ Chair
___ Business Cards   ___ Pens
___ Large plastic cup for drinking water   ___ Light
___ Copy of Sales Tax Permit (if required)   ___ Tissues
___ Trash Receptacle or bag

GENERAL
___ Professional Sign for booth or table   ___ Blank Paper
___ Tripod on which to mount sign   ___ Table Cloth
___ Clock   ___ Card or Folding Table
___ Beeper   ___ Chairs
___ Decorations for booth   ___ Paper Clips
___ Information Handouts   ___ Receipt Book
___ Business Cards   ___ Calculator
___ 2 - Plastic Business Cards Holders   ___ Writing Pad
___ Address Cards   ___ Water
___ Basket for Address Cards   ___ Products
___ Table Sign/Mailing List   ___ Signs for Products
___ Pencils (Do Not Use Pens for Schedule)   ___ Name Tags
___ Wall Hangings or Table Decorations   ___ Client Sign Up Sheet
___ Flowers for Table Decoration
___ Bank Bag or cash box
___ Change-$20's, $10's, $5's, $1's, and coin if selling products
___ Extra flyers for upcoming workshops by reader
___ Business Check with which to pay assistant

PSYCHIC FAIR LECTURE
___ Walkman and Speakers for Meditation
___ Music Tapes
___ Batteries (C and AA)
___ Handouts for particular lecture (60)
___ Pencils (30)
___ Specifics for lecture-hand stencil, grease board/markers/eraser
___ Notes for lecture

Parties and Other Public Functions

Doing psychic work at parties, festivals or public functions provides a great way to connect with a segment of the population you might otherwise never have encountered in your professional capacity. I have donated my time for occasional non-profit or charity events and I have worked for a fee at private parties, receptions, individual corporate functions and conventions.

You need to formulate an idea about what your fee or hourly rate will be for a paid event. I charge my regular hourly office-visit rate for the actual time I am reading at local events, and do not charge for travel time. Some readers give a discount from their normal hourly rate and may or may not charge for travel. With out-of-town jobs you need to decide whether you need to charge for some travel time if it will significantly take time away from your normal daily productivity, or if the travel is expensive or inconvenient.

When a call comes to my office from a client asking me to do an event, I first determine if they are comfortable with my fee. Next, I need to know a number of things about the event. The following are 20 questions I ask the caller:

1. The caller's name and phone numbers?

2. The date and hours of the event?

3. The location of and directions to the event and how long will it take to get there?

4. Who is giving the party?

5. What is the occasion?

6. Who will be at the party? (Age, gender, professions, general public, or other distinguishing characteristics.)

7. How big is the facility, how may people will be attending, and how many will participate in the readings?

8. How long should each reading be? For example, approxi-

mately 15 people can be seen in one hour doing four-minute readings, but only 12 can be seen doing five-minute readings.

9. Will alcohol be served? Heavy consumption of alcohol, especially over the course of the event, can significantly affect the emotional response and comprehension of the clients. Also, I never imbibe before or during an event. It is important to maintain focus and clarity in dealing with clients.

10. What sort of entertainment is planned? Are there other psychic readers, games, cutting of cake and presents, a band or stereo with dancing?

11. What will the noise level be? If you do readings next to the band, I can almost guarantee you will be hoarse and maybe even a little hard of hearing by the end of the event.

12. Will there be a more private or secluded place in which to do readings?

13. Will a table or chairs be provided?

14. Will there be lighting or an outlet for a lamp or other necessary equipment for the readings?

15. Will there be any refreshments available? You need to know if you should eat before you arrive. I generally request that water and juice be provided for me during the event.

16. How will the readings be organized? Will there be a sign-up sheet or will people just stand in line?

17. Will there be a helper from the party who will manage the reading schedule? From my experience, if you have to wait to look for people who have signed up, your time-productivity will be altered. That's great if you're being paid by the hour and you are allowed to just keep going, but it is very difficult if the party's host expects you to see everybody by the agreed-upon time limit, if you have limited time, or another engagement following the event.

18. If more people want readings, or a readings manager is not present, whom do you contact at the event about extending the work time at the same fee rate? If you are doing well and the word gets out, people at a large event will probably come at the end of your work time and say "just one more," "just do me," or "can you fit me in?" If there are only one or two people left at the end I often see them and then pack it up. If five or ten are lined up I say,"I need to check with (whoever) and see if they want me to extend."

If "whoever" says "no," I return and say, "I'm terribly sorry, but my time is over, please feel free to take one of my cards," or "Well, I'll see one (two) more people and then I need to go." If you stay for one or two extra people, you then need to thank everyone and politely prepare to go.

19. Will it be possible to have an area to place business cards, flyers and mailing list cards, where event-goers can see them?

20. Who will be paying you, when, and how? For example, will you be paid by cash or a check at the end of the evening (which I recommend), or by a check in the mail? If the readings are "pay as you go" and someone else will collect for you, contact them before you begin the readings to make sure all the arrangements are understood.

At the end of the event always thank the event planner for their assistance. If you hang around and "schmooze" with the clients, remember to maintain your professional demeanor and try not to be flippant. Your clients will still be remembering everything you told them about themselves. You do not want to give the impression that you are not taking them or your work seriously. Some of your clients may even feel confused, vulnerable or afraid.

Doing Lectures and Group Presentations

If you have an inclination to do public speaking or presentations, those avenues give an additional opportunity for you to gain not only exposure and name recognition, but in many cases future clients. If you are accepting an invitation to speak, you need to consider many of the same factors mentioned in previous chapters. If you are asked to present a specific topic, inquire as to the nature of the event, the audience and how much time you will have.

You need to be able to adapt your material to the expectations and needs of the group, and I have experienced some interesting audiences. For example, I once was asked to give a palmistry presentation to an organization whose members all were recovering from strokes. They were a wonderful and attentive group, but having been a speech pathologist several years before, I knew not to speak too rapidly and not to get bogged down with long explanations of metaphysical minutiae.

I also was once asked to do a 20-minute talk about being a professional psychic for my daughter's 5th grade class on parent's career day. I tried to be up-beat and entertaining. I gave examples of my experiences, interpreted some of the students' clothing and jewelry, and looked at a few of their hands. The kids really seemed to enjoy the unusual aspects of my topic.

On another occasion I was invited to do a seminar on palmistry and meditation for a men's group at a federal prison. The group members were amazingly positive and I enjoyed making the presentation. However, I had to remind myself about the participants' unique situation, and not make comments such as, "You can go to any New Age book store and buy this."

I did one presentation at a school for the blind. I decided to use a psychometry exercise with Braille writing. I had the students each silently come up with their own two-choice question and punch each choice onto a separate piece of paper. They then folded the pieces of paper and exchanged papers. I led them in a guided meditation to feel, imagine or hear their spirit guides. I then had them hold the two choices from their classmate, one paper in each hand, and asked them to feel which choice was best for the other person. Upon completing the meditation, they returned the papers and pointed out and explained why one choice was the best. The students then opened the paper and discovered which was their best choice. They enjoyed the process and were fascinated by the best choices they gave and received.

Whatever the opportunity, again remember to get permission to bring business cards, flyers or other information to hand out to interested attendees. It is always good P.R. to publicly acknowledge and thank the host, officers, staff members and teachers who invited you.

Classes and Workshops

Classes or workshops can be great for adding another dimension to your individual client practice. You first need to determine your areas of expertise, and then formulate ideas about how you could present those areas in interesting and informative ways. In addition, you need to decide what length of class or workshop would be appropriate. You many wish to do 90-minute to three-hour daytime or evening classes, half-day or all-day workshops, or a multiple-day or weekend workshop. The length may be dependent upon several factors, such as your own level of teaching or public speaking experience; the size, cost and location of the classroom space; the size and interest-level of the attendee market; the cost of appropriate advertising; and whether or not you will be presenting alone or in conjunction with other presenters or other activities.

If you are considering working on your own, I recommend starting with an approximately two-hour program which can be held either during the day, or in the early evening after normal working hours. You need to find a meeting space which is as inexpensive as possible, and that has parking and some degree of safety. The venue should have bathroom facilities, heating and air conditioning and some way of obtaining water or drinks for attendees. Chairs are important, and tables, grease boards, a microphone with amplifier, and lights on a dimmer control are also nice to have. You can use your own home if you are not anticipating a huge initial turn out. Office suite conference rooms, vacant offices, church meeting rooms, holistic practitioner's clinics, hotel meeting rooms and private school spaces may also work.

When you find a likely venue, depending upon your familiarity with the owner of the space, and how much time, energy and money you are putting on the line, you might want to get a written contract, letter or agreement to use the space at the agreed-upon time and date. The dates of your classes and workshops depend upon your own schedule, the dates the specific spaces are available, and trying to determine when your students would most likely be able to attend.

I do my own readings on my potential class dates in order to find dates with the best energy, and have had pretty good overall success, although I too have had my misses and surprises. I once scheduled a workshop at a hotel on a date which unfortunately coincided with the arrival of an ice storm. So, I ended up giving a two-hour workshop for three people. On the other hand, I have had packed houses on dates with severe thunderstorms, and I once was guided to do a workshop on Super Bowl Sunday, and had an amazingly good turn-out. You just never know, so learn to trust your guidance.

You can determine the fee for your class by learning what is being charged for other similar presentations in the local area, and ask what feels right. I generally give attendees a price break if they send money in advance, with a slightly higher fee if they pay at the door. With most workshops I give a credit or refund if a student pays in advance but cannot attend. An exception would be in the case of a longer term class with a higher tuition and a limited number of students. In that instance I state in the flyer that refunds will be given only up to a certain date, which is usually a few days prior to the first session.

My rule of thumb about whether or not a workshop is purely a financial success relates to whether the total receipts exceed the sum of the cost of the space, all overhead expenses incurred and the amount I would have received for working the same period of time with individual clients. However, even if the receipts do not exceed the sum of the above factors, classes are great for the intangibles of advertising, exposure and name recognition, which will all pay off in the long run.

Advertising is important for the success of your class. If the venue has an appropriate organizational newsletter, consider advertising in it. You should make up a catchy (but professional) flyer, send it out to your mailing list, and make it available to clients where you do your work. I have included a sample workshop flyer in Figure 1. Whether you post the flyers yourself or use a mailing service, plan to have distribution at least two to three weeks prior to the first class. That will give prospective students time to consider attending and make the necessary schedule adjustments.

Once you know the classes, dates, times, and have the advertising in motion, it's time to work on the details. If you anticipate a significant number of students, you may want to arrange for a volunteer or paid helper to assist in arranging furniture, greeting students and taking money, handing out materials, checking the thermostat, selling products, and many other useful "go-fer" activities. In most of my workshops I find helpers to be invaluable.

I recommend making, in advance, an outline of your presentation which also contains house-keeping information such as where the bathrooms are and where smoking is permitted at breaks, and an introduction which give attendees an idea of what to expect in the workshop. Additionally, you should have a personal checklist which includes a list of necessary equipment and supplies, such as chairs, markers with grease board, sound system with music, extra pencils and paper, business cards and flyers, handouts and visual aids, water, juice, disposable cups, products for sale, receipt books and an extension cord. Also remember to bring a money container and change if you plan on accepting cash.

I suggest checking out your venue in advance, if at all possible. Make sure you will get a key or access to the space on the class night, and get the phone number of an official contact to call regarding questions or mishaps. Check for things like the number of chairs available, the location of electrical outlets, the availability of a telephone, how to operate the lighting or thermostat, and how to lock up at the conclusion of the presentation. Most hosts are very helpful and will probably be relieved by your obvious professionalism and thoroughness in doing this advance planning.

You should arrive at least one hour early at the workshop space and begin setting up. If you have a helper, delegate authority and turn them loose. I prefer to assist with set up, but then 10 to 15 minutes before the beginning of the class, I turn it over to the helper and retire to another room to collect my thoughts and go over my outline. Then I can emerge, hopefully fresh and focused on the activities to come.

During the class or workshop remember to stay tuned in to the temperature comfort level of the group and build in a break or two so individuals may make a bathroom pit stop, or take a moment to stretch their legs. I like to keep my classes as light and interactive as possible to inspire the receptivity and openness of the students. For some presentations I hand out anonymous evaluation forms at the end of the session and ask attendees to give me feedback by answering a few questions about their impressions of the workshop.

Overall, I have found classes and workshops to be very instrumental in supporting my work, and I will probably continue to do them in one form or another. I also try to keep in mind a saying in the Kuan-Tzu, a fourth-century book of Chinese proverbs: "If you give a man a fish he eats a single meal. If you teach a man to fish he eats a lifetime." I think teaching people how to open up spiritually and metaphysically helps them to help themselves, and is an intrinsically worthwhile pursuit.

Audio Cassettes and Compact Discs

I have been in the process of producing a series of what I call psychic development tapes. Tapes and C.D.'s are great ways to reach people with your work and provide you with additional advertising. If you are able to market and distribute the merchandise avidly, you can also create a small side income once you recover your production costs.

If you decide to do a tape or C.D., I recommend determining

initially what your skill areas are and what subject matter would lend itself to a tape. Then try out the material on friends, individual clients or in workshops. As you hone your presentation skills, do practice tapes, and time and transcribe the contents.

You may need to have background music. If you cannot produce your own music, find a musician who is willing to provide you with a suitable background composition. Listen to the music to determine suitability, and don't be afraid to give suggestions to the composer about altering the sound. They should record the music onto a digital audio tape (D.A.T.) and provide you with the tape.

I recommend getting a written contract to buy the music outright, or at least get a license to use it for your specific purposes. If you do use someone else's music, I strongly advise allocating money to retain an attorney to assist you with the music contract. It will help preclude any misunderstandings or legal problems down the road. For example, I was discouraged from granting royalties to musicians for my initial productions. I was told that if your work is relatively unknown, and if you are not able to sell a huge number of copies, the legal and bookkeeping time and expense required to pay a small royalty can be more than the profit you make from the sales of your product.

After you have clarified your verbal content, developed a script and procured appropriate music, several simple steps are involved in producing the tape or C.D. You first need to locate professionals who have studios in which to record your voice on D.A.T, mix the voice music and music, "clean-up" (delete noise from) the final composition, and fit the mixed production onto the appropriate length of tape or C.D. Studio time usually is charged by the hour.

You may then need a graphic artist to render your concept of the cover on the "J Card" (unless you can do the graphics yourself). Finally, you will need a manufacturing company that can put it all together and bulk produce the tapes in their shrink-wrapped containers suitable for sale. You may wish to consider securing an International Standard Book Number (ISBN) with bar code to place on the items to aid you in marketing them to retail stores. The manufacturing company representative can probably assist you with information.

You will need to check with your state government about procuring a sales tax permit, if one is necessary. You would then need to determine what paperwork and record keeping would be required in order to file state or local sales tax for the proceeds of your merchandise. You can also check with your tax professionals about how to calculate production costs and how to report yearly beginning and ending inventories.

To assist in marketing, produce display ads and flyers. Also invest in Plexiglas stands or displays to show off your tapes anywhere you work or travel. You may also wish to contact distributors of similar material to see if they will pick up your productions for regional or national distribution. Hopefully, all will go well and your sales will exceed your production costs.

Books

The contents of this section are a work in progress. This being my first book-length publishing effort, I talked to a number of people in the publishing field or who had published their own books. The advice I received for a first effort is to self-publish. Getting a major publisher to accept the initial work of an unknown author can be a long shot. If you can write, edit, proof, layout, design the cover and print the book yourself, great! If not, you may need to shop around and find skilled or even professional people to whom you can subcontract these tasks.

Other guidance suggests not skimping on the cover and using a local printer so you can monitor quality and reduce shipping costs. It is also my understanding that anything you can do to advertise and market your own book will help it to be picked up by wholesale distributors who contract to supply the mass retail markets. Good luck on this one.

I'll let you know how my project works out.

Out of Town Work

Going out of town to do presentations and readings can broaden your clientele and give you a chance to travel. Some professionals work hard to find opportunities in places they'd like to visit. I, on the other hand, have tended to wait for doors to open before walking through them. I have waited until opportunities or individuals present themselves to host me.

However you decide to accept work out of town, I recommend that you determine how many people will be attending the event and in what activities you will be engaged. Inquire as to the availability of any comfortable accommodations with your hosts which might be free or inexpensive. If the event is a presentation, ask about the size of the space, the location, and the availability of parking. If you are doing individual sessions ask about a free (or inexpensive), accessible, comfortable place to read or work.

When designing your schedule, remember to check the local rush hour traffic patterns, and build in time for breaks and food. If your main focus will be individual sessions, you also may want to consider offering a free introductory lecture or demonstration of your work at the beginning of your visit. You can coordinate that with the host. If possible, provide the host with a schedule and fee information and let them schedule and confirm clients (including current phone numbers) in advance. I usually offer a complimentary consultation to the venue host and the accommodation host if they are helping me for free.

In preparing for your trip, always make a packing list which includes not only personal items, but also your professional equipment and information. In some cases it may be easier to bring master copies of flyers or other items and reproduce them at your destination than to haul around a bunch of bulky boxes.

Working Out of the Country

Planning the logistics for working outside of the country is even more important than when you are working nationally. After confirming that you have a firm offer to work internationally, make sure you have the name and phone number of a "reachable" contact person and/or organization to help coordinate your visit. Determine the time difference and call the contact person at an appropriate local time, well in advance, to iron out details.

Inquire about any language or communication requirements. If you are multilingual, excellent — as long as you can communicate with the local folks, whether in Spanish for Latin America or French in Quebec. When I worked in Hong Kong, about two-thirds of my clients were English-speaking westerners, and one-third were Chinese, the majority of whom were Cantonese-speaking with English as a second language. In some cases the Chinese clients who could not speak English brought interpreters. For the most part, the communications went fine, but there are definite differences in semantics and idioms between different countries and cultures where supposedly the same language is spoken. For example, in Australia a "napkin" is a baby diaper and in England a pencil eraser is called a "rubber." The more personal experience and local help you have, the better.

Determine the mode and cost of transportation to your destination. There are a lot of options and you should check newspapers and travel agencies for the best deals. Also, check passport and visa requirements in advance, and make sure your visa covers the entire length of time you are planning to stay. Take extra photocopies of your passport, driver's license, birth certificate or even voter registration in case the originals are lost or stolen. You might also want to bring two extra passport photos just in case.

Determine where you will be staying during your visit. Double check that your accommodations will be conveniently near where you will be working, or that available transportation will allow you sufficient mobility to get to and from the required locations. Staying with your local contacts is often the best bet. But hotels or inns can be great, depending upon their cost and whether or not you can sufficiently recharge your emotional and physical energy in them.

Check on the state of the local economy and ask advice about what fees to set for your services. For example, you might be able to ask more for your services in Hong Kong or Tokyo than in Bombay or Manila. Familiarize yourself with the local currency and exchange rate. You might even want to carry a conversion table.

If possible, obtain some local currency before you arrive. You may need it for transportation, personal items and even change for your first readings, if you arrive when the banks are not open. I know about this from first hand experience. I once arrived in Hong Kong on a Sunday morning with work to do Monday morning. I was grateful that I had thought to change some money before I left the U.S.

The usual foreign travel advice applies here. Don't flash your cash, valuables or documents, and when in developing countries I recommend using a money belt if you expect to be walking in crowded public places. I suggest arriving with and leaving the country with money in U.S. traveler's checks for security and safety. They are also easier to replace if stolen.

Find out if you need 110v/220v adapters for your appliances or recording equipment. Remember too that 220 volt outlets differ greatly from country to country. Get the appropriate adapters before you go. In developing countries electrical power surges occasionally, so bring an extra cassette recorder or whatever you feel is professionally indispensable to your work. On my first trip to Hong Kong my primary cassette recorder blew out on the second day of a two-week trip, but luckily I had a spare with me. Batteries are good, but can get bulky and expensive if you are using electronic equipment for several days straight.

I also suggest taking batteries out of electronic equipment before you pack them in your bags. Once, while checking in my baggage at the airport as I prepared to leave Hong Kong, the x-ray attendant demanded that I open my tightly packed large suitcase because it contained pieces of electronic equipment with batteries in them. I certainly appreciated the anti-terrorist precautions, but unfortunately the latch on my suitcase then broke and my bag was sent from Hong Kong to Los Angeles held together only by two thick nylon straps. Oh well. Amazingly, nothing fell out, but my belongings were really cold when I picked up my bag at LAX.

Decide well in advance what you need in the way of equipment or supplies, and inquire as to the availability and reliability of those items at your destination. When in serious doubt, take your own. Bring plenty of business cards, flyers and other personal information, as well as copies of handouts if you are doing presentations. Bring any hard to produce visual aids, your music tapes and possibly a walkman with portable speakers for a sound system. If you use or sell video tapes, make sure your system is the same as in the destination country. In Hong Kong and England for example, the PAL system is used, whereas the U.S. uses NTSC.

If you have food restrictions, find out what is available where you are going. Some national cuisines can easily accommodate vegetarian or specific diets, while others cannot. Bring some of your necessities with you if you can, just in case. Take some bottled water with you for the trip, and possibly iodine or other water purification tablets if you anticipate traveling in the boon-docks or in a developing country.

Learn in advance about any medical dangers in your destination country. Get shots and prescriptions before you leave. Take an extra pair of glasses or contacts and a copy of your eye prescription.

It's easy to get bogged down with all of the planning and preparation of international travel. But remember to savor the experience — the sights, the sounds, the food, local dress and culture. Make sure you bring your camera and don't forget to buy some souvenirs. Have a great trip!

6

PSYCHICS AND MONEY

Overcoming Problems Psychics Have in Receiving Money

People may say "I want to make money, be abundant, get rich," etc., but that doesn't mean they will make money. Making money is not related to how smart or talented we are, how hard we work, or whether or not we are a nice person. We all know people who seem to make (and keep) a lot of money who are not particularly smart or talented, who do not work hard, or who do not appear to be nice. Financial abundance is related to how much we are ready to express our gifts and talents in the world, and how much material reward we are subconsciously ready to receive in return.

Psychics are not always grounded, that is, able to stay focused on daily, practical or business requirements. Some psychics may also have a poverty consciousness, whereby they have a subconscious fear of financial success, or somewhere in their self-concept is a feeling of unworthiness about receiving abundance.

A psychic could be motivated to give every ounce of their energy to help others. But, if a professional psychic is not grounded in practicality, or if they are subconsciously not ready to receive, they can be sabotaging themselves and will not do the right things to be able to attract and receive money.

As I mentioned before, I did readings for 17 years before I allowed myself to accept money for my work. A lot of people feel, whether through belief, religious interpretation or fear, that it is not permissible to accept remuneration for metaphysical work. I hold another view.

My own comfort with receiving money as a psychic hinges on three general beliefs: that psychic ability is a talent which one can receive money for; that it is okay to charge what one's time is worth in the market place; and that money is a form of energy which meets the requirement of a valid energy exchange between the reader and client.

First, psychic or healing abilities are gifts not unlike any other gifts in the earth plane. Helping others through accurate psychic impressions or helping others heal are talents potentially as worthy of pay as being able to throw a football 70 yards on Sunday afternoon or paint a beautiful picture. The psychic path is the avenue I feel I have been given to express God's Light and to provide for my family.

My second precept is that I charge for my time, not for my gift. I use the professional model for my practice much like a psychologist, therapist or lawyer. If information I give a client calms or encourages them, or if they make a million dollars with it, the fee is the same. In contrast, I don't use a sales model for my practice, and don't give percentage reductions, discounts or kickbacks to referral sources. Apart from the ethical problems of those transactions, given that 90% of my business comes from word-of-mouth, trying to keep track of all the percentages or discounts could be a bookkeeping nightmare. As a reader or practitioner you may wish to consider fee structures which include tithing, scholarships, donations, pro-rata reductions, or delayed or incremental payment for clients with fewer resources. Think about what you are most comfortable with, and make these decisions prior to working with your clientele.

My third tenet is that the Earth is an energetic plane, and is a system of energy flow and exchange. On another level I experience all living things as balls of multi-colored energy. James Redfield focuses at length on this concept of energy and interactive flow between plant, animal and of course the human entities in his book, *The Celestine Prophecy: An Adventure*. We are constantly giving and receiving energy on many levels. When we do psychic work or healing effectively, gifts of energy are given to our clients.

If someone gives out energy in loving, healing, helping, creating, entertaining, being generous or through some other mode, they must also receive from other beings (or from the universe) a return of energy to maintain health and stability. The return of energy may be in the form of money, love, appreciation, approval, acceptance, care, support, protection, healing, or something else that is meaningful. In the case of being a professional psychic, the receipt of money can supply balance in the energetic equation.

Using the example of an electrical circuit, imagine that a giving, helping or care-taking person is energetically connected to the receiving individual or situation by two wires, a sending wire and a receiving wire. If the giver supplies energy through the sending wire (as in doing a reading), but has disconnected or refuses to accept returning energy (money or support) through the receiving wire, then there is no current in the electrical circuit. (See Figure 5)

The giver can put 250,000 volts worth of positive helping potential in the direction of the receiver, but if the giver does not receive in turn (in other words metaphysically holding the wire with a rubber glove), there is no current or "amperage" in the circuit. You may hear a loud static "pop," but no real work is done. Both the giver and receiver must receive. If only the re-

Figure 5

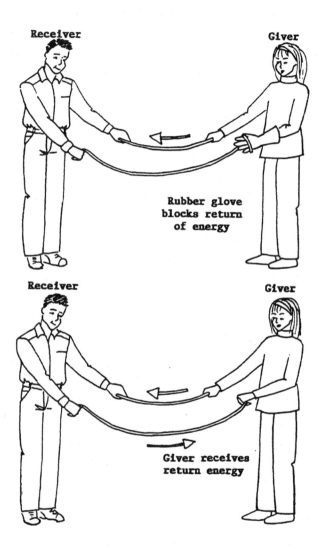

ceiver is open, the helping act may look good on the surface, but neither the giver nor the receiver will be able to gain maximum benefit from the exchange.

From a practical standpoint, several difficulties can arise from an imbalanced energy equation. For one thing the minimized energy exchange can manifest itself in the client being less likely to recognize lasting positive results and therefore not returning, or not referring others. Another problem with an invalid energy exchange is that the practitioner who does not receive enough can create what I call a "leak in their own boat," energetically speaking. I believe the universe is always reflecting back to each of us the composite of what we are doing or not doing on our own behalf. If we give continually to others, but for reasons such as guilt or low self concept we are unable to receive a commensurate amount of energy in return, we are in a sense "ripping ourselves off." Usually, over a period of time, the universe will reflect back to us what we are doing, and we can manifest our own experience of being cheated in the daily world, or attracting what some people refer to as bad luck. This can of course affect us both financially and professionally.

In other words, we need to receive for two important reasons. First, we need to validate our relationship with our clients and be willing to receive so that they benefit maximally (and our business prospers, too). Second, we need to honor our own inner child and receive what our services are worth in the marketplace (or some other commensurate package of exchange), or we will create an energy "self-rip-off" which the universe will reflect to us in some tangible way.

Why People Will Pay a Lot of Money For Psychic Work

Aspiring psychics need to know that the psychic field presently has a lot going for it. Well-marketed and accurate psychic work constitutes a personal service that can command a relatively high rate of return. Over the years, I have found that people will pay hard currency for a variety of situations, which I have listed below. I will explain how psychic work fits each of these categories. They are as follows:

1. Doing the unusual or something no one else does (e.g., playing Beethoven on trash can lids).

2. Providing entertainment (e.g., virtually anything).

3. Solving problems (e.g., virtually anything).

4. Saving or making money (self-explanatory).

5. Giving people something or some experience they feel they really want (e.g., toy, car, boat, food, clothing, cosmetics, fun, help, relief).

6. Giving them something they think will make them feel better or be happier (physically, emotionally, mentally or spiritually).

7. Being noted as one of the best at something, whatever that is (e.g., champion tidly-wink player).

When doing readings, bear in mind that professional psychics already do something that most people don't do (#1). Individuals also enjoy learning about themselves, so in that sense a reading is entertaining (#2). If your psychic modality looks at present or future situations and gives clients opportunity to make more informed decisions, you are problem solving and often helping them to make or save money (#3, #4). If your assistance is seen to be accurate, then you build credibility and your clients will return willingly, believing that your assistance will give them an edge for success or happiness in their life, as well as a sense of empowerment and well-being (#5, #6).

As for reason #7, "being one of the best at something," bear in mind that if you are already doing psychic readings for money, you are a professional and in that sense already considered one of the best relative to amateur psychics and the general population. As professional psychics (or healers), I feel we should all aspire to be the best channel of Light for our clients' highest good that we can, and not focus on being a "great psychic" or "gifted healer." But, on the other hand, if we do receive compliments, kudos, air mentions, media attention or make documented on-target predictions, it is okay to honor that positive feedback for our channel and publicize it tastefully. It gives prospective clients more information in their decision-making about scheduling an appointment.

7 MANIFESTING MONEY

One of my speech pathology professors used to quote his grandfather in saying, "Talk is cheap, but it takes money to buy whiskey." Over the years I have observed the attitudes and behaviors of scores of my clients who are financially successful. I have tried to learn all I could about how to mix the daily conscious world with esoteric pursuits in a fruitful manner. I have devised four major rungs on the ladder of manifesting financial abundance that have worked well for me.

During the past 15 years, of my clients who claim to have used these techniques faithfully, approximately four out of every five (80%) report receiving some financial gain or career success that they had no reason to expect — within a mere two weeks after initiating the techniques. Examples include unexpected job offers, winning money at the supermarket, winning a raffle, receiving a check from an insurance company, an early inheritance from a parent, a surprise birthday party at the hairdresser (it wasn't even her birthday), an individual receiving three debt repayments in the same week, someone being loaned $15,000 worth of photographic equipment for a project, and on and on.

I am not always sure why 20% do not seem to experience a surprise gain, but there are probably a variety of factors involved including lessons about faith, astrological timing, unconsciously rigid adherence to a poverty consciousness, or abundance fears. Nevertheless, the majority of my clients have noted success with this particular process, and it cannot hurt to try it. The four steps to abundance are as follows:

1. Reprogramming Childhood (or Even Past-Life) Attitudes About Money. I grew up hearing all kinds of judgmental statements which gave money value, like, "Money doesn't grow on trees," "Money is the root of all evil," "That old boy is worth two million," and in more recent years, "Money talks and B.S. walks." In fact, money has no value other that which we attach to it. It is neither positive nor negative. It has nothing to do with how hard we work, how smart or talented we are, or whether or not we are a nice person.

Money is merely a translational form of energy. Money is conveyed as a result of the giver's and receiver's shared beliefs about perceived value. In its physical state money represents potential energy. When it is conveyed, it kinetically translates into goods, services, perceived choices, a sense of freedom, an association with or feeling of power, and many other experiences.

As stated in the previous chapter, money is simply a product of (1) projecting enthusiastically to the world, the interests, talents and gifts that we have been given in this life, and (2) our subconscious and conscious willingness to receive an equivalent amount of energy in return. When we can achieve those two states, I believe money inevitably follows. We need to catch ourselves playing the old childhood money tapes in our daily mind-chatter, cancel them out, and substitute a positive affirmation.

Examples include changing the judgment "Money doesn't grow on trees," to "Abundance is available to me everywhere," or the judgment "Money is the root of all evil," to "It is safe to have money because it is neither good nor evil, and it is merely energy which can be used positively." Remember also to be vigilant in ferreting out the subtle feelings and fears that usually go along with money value judgments. Those emotions can make the attitudes more powerful and potentially more tricky to transmute. Deep breathing, breathwork or healing energy work may help in the release process.

2. Donating or Tithing (For the Right Reasons).

Many metaphysicians, wealthy individuals and wealthy metaphysicians have long recognized the power of tithing. To me this means giving *away* some portion of your income (not necessarily 10%), regularly and gratefully, to somewhere that spiritually nurtures you. Some people suggest that volunteer time can be tithing. If you are someone like Bill Gates who has more money than time, then time may be a significant donation. If on the other hand, like most of the rest of us, you have more time than money, then you should probably kick in the bucks.

Donating usually needs to be to a charity or religious situation with which we are in alignment, not to a relative, friend or another individual. If we give to an individual, we run the risk of creating a debtor power imbalance. In other words, they may become resentful about our being in a financial position above them, or may emotionally give their "power" away to us by seeing us as the necessary rescuer and themselves as helpless. Also, if we bail someone out by paying their debts or rent or whatever, we can be unknowingly be "putting gasoline on their fire" and contributing to the continuation of their self doubt, or difficulty in taking responsibility for solving their own problems. That is not to say that we should let someone starve if we have the wherewithal to feed them. But, we should facilitate their empowerment whenever possible by not rescuing where it does not seem appropriate.

I also encourage people not to earmark or control the donation, but to release dominion over it. For example, someone might say, "I'll donate this much money to your charity, but you have to use it for buying a new building." That might be great unless there is not enough money to pay staff or buy materials. Someone else might say, "Well, I won't give you money, but I'll bake you a chocolate cake instead." The sentiment may seem wonderful, but what if the recipients of the cake are sugar addicts, chocoholics or diabetics? Controlling the donation can create a counterproductive result on all levels.

The giving should also be for the right reason, which I believe is the realization that donating is merely servicing the cosmic abundance machine, greasing its wheels and adding motor oil to its engine. If we have hidden agendas, like getting a good tax write-off, winning respect from society, or buying a better ticket to Heaven, we might mitigate the positive effect of the donation. Likewise, if someone has not paid their debt to us and we say, "That's okay, I'll just call it a tithe," that's not really tithing. What actually happened was we just got ripped off.

3. Finding and Doing Our Dharmic Path or Right Livelihood in the World.

Each person follows their own singular and unique path in their lifetime. There are also for each of us a number of events and lessons which our higher self has agreed for us to experience along the way. Those lessons may include experiencing patience, assertiveness, cooperation, independence, creativity, service, practical survival, spiritual searching, protecting or defending, building in the physical world, parenting, and an infinite number of others.

Sometimes our lessons are connected directly to a specific vocation and we feel it at a very early age. Often, though, our right livelihood seems to be the result of a progression from one vocational arena to another. I believe that however aimless we feel, our progression from one career to the next is actually a part of our path, and that we gain wisdom, accomplish lessons, heal and advance spiritually with each new career direction. I also have seen many clients, including myself, who are on a path of trust and faith, where we must march into the unknown future without guarantees. Being a pioneer, ground breaker, explorer or vanguard without a comfortable set pattern to follow is what some of us get to experience.

I personally received some general life guidance when I was about 14 years old. I was feeling very depressed, crying in my room and asking repeatedly, "What am I here for, what am I on Earth for?" After about 10 minutes, it felt as though a psychic tunnel opened up to my head, and a deep male voice said loudly, "To help other people!" I startled, and the tunnel seemed to close quickly. I gained composure and thanked Whoever it was for the message. I have always tried to help people, but unfortunately for me it took four unfulfilling professions before I finally felt compelled, in my late 30's, to embrace my present psychic practice — which is my own right livelihood. Even with guidance and motivation, it was a huge leap of faith. I had no guarantees. For some of us, our true path includes learning to trust and have faith. I've never regretted taking the jump and things have worked out great.

So don't be discouraged if it takes awhile to find your niche. Try to be flexible and patient. Being a part-time professional psychic as you transition slowly out of your day career may, in fact, be a part of your progression.

There are practical steps to searching for your right path. They include prayer, asking for guidance in dreams, using affirmation and visualization techniques, getting psychic readings, seeking professional career advice, taking interest tests, and listening for the same guidance coming from different or unrelated areas of your life.

One affirmation-visualization technique I give clients is first to surround yourself with protective Light and imagine a fulfilling future career environment in front of you. Then affirm "Thank you God (Light or other Deiform) for smoothing a path before me in this and all other things." Imagine any obstacles being removed between yourself and the fulfilling situation, and feel the successful career experience moving effortlessly toward you. This technique will in effect be drawing the fulfilling situation closer to you, as in the Zen concept, "The target hits the arrow."

During the 17 years I was hopping careers and doing psychic readings for free, I also tried taking aptitude and interest tests. One test I took back in the olden days suggested I should consider being either a Y.M.C.A. recreation director or a Catholic priest. Not being particularly athletic and being neither Catholic nor comfortable with organized religion, those insights did not help. Another interest test said I had attitudes somewhat in common with speech pathologists. I pursued that field and was one for about six years. In those days, there was no category for professional psychic, but that is what I now feel comfortable with and best suited for.

If you have heard for years that you should be a counselor, and your hunches and knowledge of people are uncanny, or you have precognitive dreams that come true, maybe you really are psychic. If you know who is on the phone when it rings, or empathically feel the emotions or difficulties of people from a distance, or messages or words continue to leap off at you from the television or billboards and the messages turn out to be predictive, maybe you have what it takes and should consider a psychic career.

4. Using Appropriate Affirmation/Visualization Techniques Regularly.

Here is a technique to assist us in loving our inner child and helping us to feel worthy of receiving.

Imagine a gentle giant female guardian angel rocking and cradling you, feel her love, and say, "I deserve this loving female support, and I accept this loving female support." Then imagine a gentle giant male guardian angel rocking and cradling you, feel his love, and say, "I deserve this loving male support and I accept this loving male support."

Regular use of this technique will increase our feelings of self-worth, attract unexpected help from the world, and create a magnetic draw or symbolic landing pad for greater abundance.

The following affirmation/visualization is one I have been giving out and employing myself for many years. I have to admit I forget to say it sometimes, but it has always worked quickly for me whenever I have needed it.

Surround yourself with Light and say, "Thank you God (or Deiform) for this abundant prosperity, for my highest good, without struggle. I deserve to be abundantly prosperous, and I am now receiving."

Imagine resources pouring in all around you, and imag-

ine accepting them gratefully without qualification or reservation.

Practice these visualizations at least once daily for 10 days in a row.

8 FAMILY SUPPORT

If your partner, immediate and extended family, and close friends are all in agreement with and support your metaphysical beliefs and line of work, fantastic. If, on the other hand, you're like most of us, there is probably a partner, parent, child, relative or friend who doesn't believe in what you are doing and thinks you are wrong, misguided, weird, evil, nuts, or all of the above.

It is almost impossible to please everyone on a conscious level in any given situation. Ask any politician or sports referee. I try to honor people's rights to their own opinions and respect their space. If someone close to us gives us negative feedback or criticizes our pursuits, they are bringing up some of our issues in our reflective mirror, and we are bringing up some of theirs in their mirror. Example issues may include fear of personal rejection or abandonment, fear of public humiliation or even public execution (oh yes, for some of us), fear of connecting with our spiritual, psychic, or emotional inner self, fear of taking or abusing our own spiritual power, and fear of daring to look at our issues. In my experience, these reactions usually apply to both sides of the coin, both the rejecter and rejectee.

Recalling that we can't please everyone, we need to remember Who and What we work for, the Light, or God and hopefully not for the approval of partner, family or friends. Many of us would agree that if we make a choice to tread a certain path, and if we feel in our heart that the path is in our highest good, then it will be in the highest good of all concerned whether they like their perception of our path or not.

Our approval, worth and validation come from the beautiful bright light, which I call "God's Light" in the center of the heart chakra, which I believe is in every person that has ever lived. It is already in us. We can't feel it through approval gained from others. Our inner God's Light is the only source of fulfillment in satisfying our need for approval. Only our higher self knows what is really best for us, and if we enact our own highest plan, it will fit perfectly with the highest plans of everyone around us.

With respect to the belief systems of the significant others in our lives, the variation of the old English saying goes, "You can lead a horse to water, but you can't make him drink." This aphorism speaks to the reality that each of us has been given free will by God, and that our free will cannot be usurped by another unless we agree to that outcome on a higher level. This of course also applies to our partners, family members or friends, too. We cannot change their ideas, attitudes or directions without their acquiescence. Metaphysical beliefs are what someone personally "believes" about cosmology, regardless of how provable they hold those beliefs to be, whether theistic or atheistic.

If our partner, relative or friend does not embrace our belief system, we should honor their right to their experience of life, project love and forgiveness to them on a higher level, and make attempts to alter our own behavior to create a win/win situation. For example, you can agree to split time so that you get to do your "thing" part of the time, they get to do their "thing" part of the time, and there will also be shared experiences where you engage in mutually rewarding activities together. If a win/win cannot be achieved, then you can agree to boundary setting where certain subjects or travels are deemed "taboo" for discussion except for necessary informational questions such as, "Where will you be?" "How can I reach you?" or "When will you be back?" I have close relatives whom I consider to be very conservative Christians. One of them once commented to me that many of their friends in the congregation would consider what I do for a living to be the work of the Devil. I recall deciding at the time that rather than being self-justifying, defensive or proselytizing, I smiled, nodded, grunted mildly, and continued doing whatever it was I was doing. In that situation, in the interest of harmony, I chose not to try to change anyone's belief or justify my own, and returned to our previous social agreement not to discuss religion in family gatherings. In similar situations, such as during public presentations, I have said I usually say things like "I work for God," or "Thank God for the Bill of Rights (in the U.S. Constitution), which guarantees our rights of freedom of religious expression." This kind of response may, however, be received as defensive or confrontative by the people closest to us.

If unfortunately, your partner, relative or friend is angry or hostile about your metaphysical work or beliefs, you are probably facing them with some deeper past conflict, fear or pain within themselves. There may seem to be good reasons to stay connected to the person, such as love, family ties, money, security or children. However, a long-term intolerant spiritual mismatch can lead to personal suppression, a failure to communicate emotionally, a lack of spiritual honesty — and often someone ultimately becoming ill.

My departed father once said to me, "Sometimes things don't work out like you think." If we have tried everything we can think of over a long period of time and a painful spiritual mismatch continues, we may feel at some point like we're flogging a dead mule. We then may have to consider walking away from the family situation or friendship in order to open up to more light for our own path. If in the future as people grow and heal and there is more acceptance, tolerance or agreement, then the relationship may again continue. If not, as one door closes, others open to us.

9 CONCLUSION

It is very important to do what we love, whether we do it as a profession or as a hobby. Almost all of the professional psychics I have ever met love their metaphysical work, did it long before they got paid for it, and would probably do it now even if they did not get paid for it. It requires only a little talent, practice, interest in helping others and a bit of sensitivity in dealing with them.

Becoming a successful professional psychic in our modern world is now an achievable goal for most of us. To take the step, you first need a tad of courage to be different and a mustard seed of faith. As I have suggested in this book, your success will also be enhanced by holding a spiritual focus for your work, by practicing maintaining an abundance consciousness, by committing to ethical principles in your client-related and business affairs, and by applying sound business techniques and procedures.

Everyone has a slightly different life situation, and given the exciting uncertainties of life, we sometimes encounter surprises and have to be flexible and creative to adapt to new requirements. Nevertheless, the suggestions in this book have broad application and will work most of the time . . . and they have worked well for me.

I wish you the very best in your pursuit of professional metaphysical success. Good luck!

Joe Nicols

CONCLUSION

GLOSSARY

astrology — Predicting through charting the stars.

automatic writing — Writing or typing information received from the spirit world while the writer is in an altered state of consciousness.

card reading — Divining through reading Tarot, the regular deck or other types of cards.

channeling — In a conscious, semi-trance or trance state, receiving and conveying psychically gained information directly from specific spiritual entities.

clairaudience — Receiving auditory impressions of or about past, present or future events or individuals.

clairvoyance — Receiving visual images in the mind's eye of past, present or future events or individuals.

deiform — The choice of word that describes one's concept of a Supreme Being, eg., God, Light, Oneness, etc.

dharma — An eastern concept related to a person's life path or life duty.

discarnate spirits — Spirit beings who once occupied or could occupy physical bodies and who are present but not currently embodied.

dowsing — Finding water or minerals by "witching" with a dowsing stick, or observing the motion of a pendulum with a suspended crystal or other object.

elemental spirits or elementals — Energies which are related to the basic life force of nature which can be discretely separated from spirit form into physical form such as in the majority of animals, insects and plants.

empathy — Experiencing someone else's physical sensations and emotions as if they are occurring within one's own body.

energy vampire — A person who, due to unconscious fear, neediness or anger, or through conscious intent, draws life energy (or "chi" in Chinese medicine) from another person, causing that person to feel or become weak, fearful or angry, or to become ill.

karma — An eastern concept whereby a person's behavior or attitudes in one experience can create or attract positive or negative events or situations in a future time or future lifetime.

kinesthesia — Receiving information through body movement or positioning, or sensing the movement or body stress of others as if one is also experiencing it. Can be a type of empathy.

numerology — Gaining insight through studying the spiritual numbers derived from dates, names and places.

palmistry — Gaining psychic information through observing the lines and structures in the hand.

precognition — Knowing future events through psychic means.

psychic modality — A type of psychic receptivity related to the senses, eg., clairvoyance, clairaudience, empathy, psychometry, kinesthesia, etc.

psychometry — Obtaining information about a person or situation through holding or touching an object associated with that person or situation.

reader — An individual who uses psychic ability and techniques to relate a person's past, present and future.

Reiki — A Japanese hands-on healing technique, whereby positive life force is channeled through the healer into the body and energy field of the recipient.

scrying — Seeing events in a crystal ball.

spirit guides — Discarnate beings which may be guardian angels, ascended masters, or evolved individuals whom the person has known previously in this or a previous life, and who benevolently watches over and assists the person in their life and spiritual development.

tactile — Receiving information through touch by the fingers or hands, or other body areas.

telepathy — A psychic ability usually interpreted as the ability to read the thoughts of another individual.

thought form — An energetic creation from a person's emotions or attitudes which does not have its own consciousness, but which nonetheless can have a psychic or even physical effect on someone else.

trance channeling — Assuming an altered state and allowing a discarnate or disembodied being to speak through the psychic.

RECOMMENDED READING

Rama, Swami, Ajaya, Swami, ed. *Living With the Himalayan Masters: Spiritual Experiences of Swami Rama.* Honesdale, PN: Himalayan International Institute of Yoga Science and Philosophy of the U.S.A., 1978.

Benham, William G. *The Laws of Scientific Hand Reading: A Practical Treatise on Scientific Hand Analysis.* New York: Hawthorn Books, Inc., 1974.

Boyd, Doug. *Rolling Thunder.* New York, NY: Delta, 1974.

Bro, Ph.D., Harmon H., Hugh Lynn Cayce, ed. *Edgar Cayce On Dreams.* New York, NY: Warner Books, 1968.

Gersi, Douchan. *Faces in the Smoke: An Eye Witness Experience of Voodoo, Shamanism, Psychic Healing and Other Amazing Human Powers.* Los Angeles, CA: Jeremy P. Tarcher, Inc., 1991.

Gray, Ph.D., John. *Men Are From Mars, Women Are From Venus: A Practical Guide for Improving Communication and Getting What You Want in Your Relationships.* New York, NY: Harper Collins Publishers, 1992.

Hendrix, Ph.D., Harville. *Getting the Love You Want: A Guide For Couples.* New York, NY: Reprinted from hard cover by Henry Holt & Company, Inc., Harper Perennial, 1988.

Markides, Kyriacos C. *The Magus of Strovolos: The Extraordinary World of a Spiritual Healer.* New York, NY: Arkana, Penguin Books, Inc., 1985.

Redfield, James. *The Celestine Prophecy: An Adventure.* New York, NY: Warner Books, 1993.

Rossbach, Sarah. *Feng Shui: The Chinese Art of Placement.* New York, NY: Arkana, Penguin Books, U.S.A., Inc. 1983.

Rossbach, Sarah. *Interior Design With Feng Shui.* New York, NY: Penguin/Arkana, 1987.

Yogananda, Paramahansa. *Autobiography of a Yogi.* Los Angeles, CA: Self- Realization Fellowship, 1946.

Wilhelm, Richard (translation), rendered into English by Cary F. Baynes. *The I Ching or Book of Changes.* New York, NY: Bollinger Series XIX, Princeton University Press, 1950.

RECOMMENDED READING

ABOUT THE AUTHOR

Joe Nicols has spent over 30 years in the study of palmistry and psychic development. He has been a full-time professional psychic for 12 years.

Joe founded the Central Texas Parapsychology Association, a non-profit organization dedicated to fostering understanding of psychic phenomena. He was named the "Best Psychic in Austin" by the *Austin Chronicle*'s Readers' Poll, has appeared on radio and television, and has conducted seminars and workshops in numerous cities throughout the United States and overseas, including Hong Kong and India.

Joe offers personal consultations in which he answers questions concerning a client's career, love life, finances, health, geographic moves, travel, psychic abilities and life decisions. He has also done telephone readings for private sessions and over the radio. He teaches workshops and seminars on such topics as "Psychic Development," "Psychic Healing," "Palmistry," "Dream and Symbol Interpretations," "Discovering Past Lives," "Reading the Regular Deck of Playing Cards," "Manifesting a Better Love Life," "Manifesting a More Fulfilling Career" and "Manifesting Financial Abundance." He has also trained a number of individuals who are now working as professional psychics.

Joe brings a varied personal background to his work, including having been an Army officer and having lived and worked in Australia. He holds a Master of Arts degree in Speech-Language Pathology from the University of Texas at Austin, and has had six years of clinical experience in hospital and rehabilitation settings.

For other works by Joe Nicols, M.A.:

Tranquility Press
P.O. Box 163392
Austin, TX 78716

YES, please send me the items checked:

☐ **Psychic Development: Connecting With Your Spirit Guides — A Guided Visualization Meditation (cassette) ....$14.95 (includes S&H)**

This cassette tape is designed to assist anyone who has an interest in developing their own psychic ability, from beginners to advanced students. The techniques used are a culmination of experiences gained through over 30 years of personal questing and 14 years of professional psychic development presentations.

☐ **How To Make a Good Living as a Professional Psychic (trade paperback/111 pp.) ....$15.95 (includes S&H)**

This book offers you detailed business insights from a full-time psychic and palmist whose practice regularly grosses over $100,000 annually. Designed for anyone considering full- or part-time professional psychic work, it will benefit a wide range of metaphysical and holistic professionals, including massage therapists, healers and energy workers.

☐ **Special! Please send me both Joe's cassette and book for the special low price of only $24.95 (includes S&H)**

☐ Please send me more information on Joe's individual consultations.

— —

Name _____

Address _____

City _____ State _____ Zip _____

Amount Enclosed: $ _____

Allow 4-6 weeks delivery. Prices subject to change. Please do not send cash.